Better. Mental. Health. for Everyone

A publication of Recovery International Inc.
2022

BETTER. MENTAL. HEALTH. *for Everyone*

This workbook is designed to be used as a self-help manual or part of a group training session. While the Recovery International (RI) Method often serves as an adjunct to professional care, it is not a substitute for therapy, counseling or medical advice. If you believe you need such counseling or advice, contact a mental health or health care professional.

Better. Mental. Health.™ for Everyone

© 2022 Recovery International

All rights reserved. No portion of this workbook may be reproduced, stored in a retrieval system, or transmitted in any form or by any means – electronic, mechanical, photocopy, recording, scanning or other – except brief quotations in critical reviews or articles, or as specifically allowed by US Copyright Act of 1976, without the prior written permission of the copyright owner.

Published by:
    Recovery International
    1415 W. 22nd Street – Tower Floor
    Oak Book, IL 60523
    recoveryinternational.org

ISBN: 978-1-7342697-6-5

Printed in the United States of America

Table of Contents

Course Goals & Purpose	1
Self-Endorsement	3
Seven Keys	4
Lesson 1: Explore Main Concepts	7
Lesson 2: Recovery International Language	21
Lesson 3: Identifying Trivialities	29
Lesson 4: Build Will-Power	37
Lesson 5: Practice the Four-Step Method	47
Lesson 6: Spot the Key Concepts	57
Lesson 7: More Key Concepts	67
Lesson 8: Join a Peer-Led Meeting	77
Appendix A: Tool Lists	83
Appendix B: Glossary of Terms	89
Appendix C: Worksheets	93
Appendix D: History of Recovery International	99
Appendix E: Books by and about Dr. Low and Recovery International	105

BETTER. MENTAL. HEALTH. *for Everyone*

Course Goals

Welcome!

We live in stressful times. This workbook is designed to provide you with coping tools for everyday situations which can trigger symptoms. It will teach you to manage anger, alleviate depression, and reduce anxiety. It will help you to lead a more peaceful and productive life.

Founded in 1937, Recovery International (RI) has helped people achieve better mental health all around the world.

> Thanks to this program, I know that I acted out because I was angry and afraid, but controlling my anger gives me more balance and a sense of accomplishment.*
>
> Marcus G., Chicago, IL

> I've had depression for seven years. I used to have panic attacks. I've been attending Recovery International meetings for two years. Now, all of these things are very much in control.*
>
> Deepak D., Pune, India

*Quotes cited throughout this book are from RI members.

Purpose

The purpose of this workbook is to help you manage symptoms and stressors of everyday life. If you follow the lessons, practice these techniques, and use these tools you will be able to:
1. Identify events that upset you.
2. Distinguish between emergency and routine events.
3. Recognize symptoms you experience when you are upset.
4. Examine your reactions to situations.
5. Use cognitive behavioral tools to help you reduce those symptoms.
6. Learn to express feelings about routine situations without temper.
7. Congratulate yourself for your efforts.

Each lesson includes readings, activities and tool lists to help you learn and practice the Four-Step Recovery International Method.

This workbook book will train you to use a variety of cognitive behavioral tools, called "spots," to control your thoughts and impulses. These "spots" were developed by neuropsychiatrist Dr. Abraham Low. Look for this face symbol which marks tools or "spots" introduced throughout the workbook.

There is a lesson on "Recovery International Language" as there are terms with a different context than what you may be used to. Along with spots, some terms are in bold text and definitions are in Appendix D.

At the end of each lesson are excerpts from one of several books by the founder of the Recovery Method, Dr. Abraham Low. You can find out more about his books in Appendix E.

All of these lessons, combined with regular practice of the concepts and Four-Step Method, will help you lead a more peaceful and productive life and achieve better mental health.

> **Fearful anticipation is often worse than the realization.**
> *- Worrying about what might happen is often worse than what does happen.*

BETTER. MENTAL. HEALTH. *for Everyone*

The Power of Self-Endorsement

Throughout this book and in Recovery Meetings, you will hear the word "endorse."

Self-endorsement is praise we give ourselves for any effort. It's like patting ourselves on the back. *We do not look for endorsement from others.* We endorse ourselves.

We endorse ourselves for *any effort* we make to control how we think and act, whether we are successful or not. We endorse for our efforts to improve our mental wellness. *We focus on effort, not results.*

What are some efforts you can endorse yourself for today?

_____

_____

_____

_____

Check off the tools that apply to your situation:

- ☐ Endorse for the effort, not just the outcome.
- ☐ Self-endorsement leads to self-respect.
- ☐ Self-endorsement creates a feeling of security.
- ☐ We endorse even our smallest efforts.

"What we teach you is to endorse your successes and to refrain from condemning your failures. An attitude of this kind permits you to accumulate a vast fund of self-endorsement."
    - Dr. Abraham Low

Endorse for using this workbook today!

Seven Keys to Better Mental Health

We all deal with the ups and downs of daily life. Here are seven key tools (or "spots") to help you right away. In this program you will learn many more tools—ways to deal with what life throws at you. All are designed to help you maintain balance and perspective during daily life.

1. **Be group-minded.** We are all part of many groups: a couple, a family unit, a group of friends, a classroom of students, a team at work, or member of a club. If we act in the best interest of the group instead of in our own self-interest, harmony is maintained by fostering a spirit of partnership.

2. **Humor is our friend, temper is our enemy.** If we can see the humor in any given situation—especially a stressful one—then it changes our outlook and response to it. We face many minor irritations every day—if we allow these to annoy us, we will get worked up and be miserable. If we refuse to let these affect us, we will control our temper and relax.

3. **Don't take yourself too seriously.** If we take ourselves too seriously, we are self-focused instead of group-minded. We will give great importance to our own thoughts and feelings, and not be able to see things objectively. Taking ourselves too seriously can come across as arrogance: acting like we know all the answers and always wanting to prove that we are right. This tends to alienate people and prevents us from hearing differing opinions.

4. **Try, fail, try, fail, try—succeed!** (Or "try, try again.") Many of our tools are common-sense sayings that we have heard throughout our lives. With practicing good mental health, there may be times when we have to concentrate on certain actions, and it may go well or it may fail. People who are learning to change behavior, such as holding down temper, need a lot of practice to help this become ingrained and automatic. So, it's important to try again, and again, until we succeed.

5. **Do things in part acts**. (Or "one step at a time.") Some jobs, activities and tasks are complex. But, if broken down into smaller steps, even large tasks become manageable. If we dread doing a big job—at work or around the house—break it up into smaller steps and congratulate (or endorse) ourselves each time we complete one of these "part acts."

6. **People do things *that* annoy us, not usually *to* annoy us.** Many of us get annoyed at other people for silly, little things. And what's worse, they seem oblivious to it. But usually it's not personal—whatever someone is doing that we find annoying is often not directed at us, it's just something they are *doing*. It's easier to let go of the frustration once we realize that it is the *action* that is bothersome, not the individual.

7. **We can't change an event, but we can change our reaction to it.** This is all about *us*—how we react to any given situation. If an event is disturbing, upsetting or alarming, *we* choose if we get upset, take it in stride, or even laugh at it. The important thing is to recognize that *we* control our reaction to whatever situation we encounter. If we can't change a friend, spouse or co-worker, we have to change our attitude toward them or the situation.

> I started attending RI so that I could better handle the stress of family members with mental health issues. I feel that it has helped me tremendously. I am able to quell the anxiety that starts as soon as I wake.
>
> Martin G., Santa Barbara, CA

Lesson 1:
Explore Main Concepts

Objectives:

- Recognize the difference between angry and fearful temper.

- Distinguish between inner environment and outer environment.

> I became a much less angry person which made a huge difference for my wife and children. I also better managed my lowered feelings so I was able to work and contribute to the family in ways I had never been able to do before. I think I became a person that was just much nicer to be around.
>
> Bob G., Phoenix, AZ

> I have much greater stability and peace in home and at work.
>
> Ian M., Detroit, MI

BETTER. MENTAL. HEALTH. *for Everyone*

Important Concept #1
"Temper" Has Two Faces

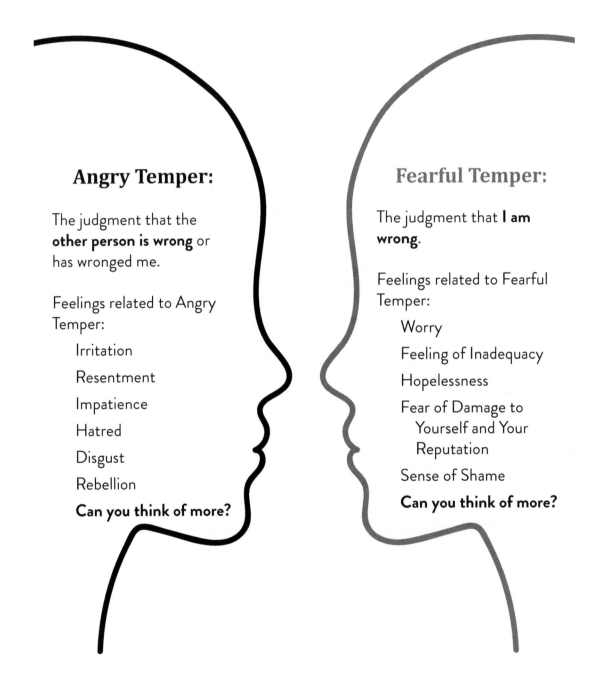

Angry Temper:

The judgment that the **other person is wrong** or has wronged me.

Feelings related to Angry Temper:

- Irritation
- Resentment
- Impatience
- Hatred
- Disgust
- Rebellion

Can you think of more?

Fearful Temper:

The judgment that **I am wrong**.

Feelings related to Fearful Temper:

- Worry
- Feeling of Inadequacy
- Hopelessness
- Fear of Damage to Yourself and Your Reputation
- Sense of Shame

Can you think of more?

© 2022 Recovery International

BETTER. MENTAL. HEALTH. *for Everyone*

Activity: Identifying Angry Temper

Write an **example of angry temper** - an everyday situation where you may have become angry, impatient, or irritated with others because you felt they were wrong or wronged you.

Situation: _____

_____

_____

Now, check off the tools that could apply to your example.

- ☐ We can assert ourselves without temper.
- ☐ We excuse rather than accuse ourselves and others.
- ☐ Humor is our best friend, temper is our worst enemy.
- ☐ We choose peace over power.
- ☐ It takes two to fight, one to lay down the sword.
- ☐ If we can't change a situation, we can change our attitude toward it.
- ☐ Calm begets calm, temper begets temper.
- ☐ We drop the judgment for our own inner peace.
- ☐ Feelings should be expressed and temper suppressed.
- ☐ Feelings are not facts.
- ☐ Every act of self-control leads to a greater sense of self-respect.
- ☐ People do things that annoy us, not necessarily to annoy us.
- ☐ We can control our speech muscles.
- ☐ We can remove ourselves from a tense and provoking situation.
- ☐ Temper is blindness to the other side of the story.
- ☐ Tempers are frequently uncontrolled, not uncontrollable.

© 2022 Recovery International

BETTER. MENTAL. HEALTH. *for Everyone*

Activity: Identifying Fearful Temper

Write an **example of fearful temper** - an everyday situation where you felt you were wrong, shameful, or were embarrassed or discouraged.

Situation: _____

_____

_____

Now, check off the tools that apply to your example.

- ☐ Humor is our best friend, temper is our worst enemy.
- ☐ We don't take ourselves too seriously.
- ☐ We excuse rather than accuse ourselves and others.
- ☐ Sensations are distressing, but not dangerous.
- ☐ There is no right or wrong in the trivialities of daily life.
- ☐ Calm begets calm, temper begets temper.
- ☐ Helplessness is not hopelessness.
- ☐ Temper maintains and intensifies symptoms.
- ☐ Endorse ourselves for the effort, not only for the performance.
- ☐ Have the courage to make mistakes.
- ☐ Fear is a belief and beliefs can be changed.
- ☐ Replace an insecure thought with a secure thought.
- ☐ Self-appointed expectations lead to self-induced frustrations.
- ☐ Decide, plan and act.
- ☐ When feeling overwhelmed, do things in "part acts."

BETTER. MENTAL. HEALTH. *for Everyone*

Important Concept
Inner and Outer "Environment"

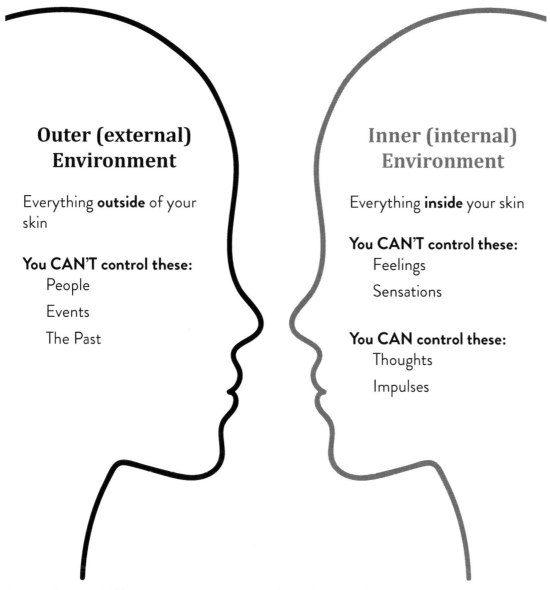

Outer (external) Environment

Everything **outside** of your skin

You CAN'T control these:
   People
   Events
   The Past

Inner (internal) Environment

Everything **inside** your skin

You CAN'T control these:
   Feelings
   Sensations

You CAN control these:
   Thoughts
   Impulses

As much as we'd like to, we cannot control our friends, family members, the person on the bus, or the woman driving next to us. We also have no control over weather, world events, the past or decisions we made in the past.

After our initial feelings and sensations during an event, we can control our thoughts and impulses and our actions and reactions to situations. In Recovery language, that is "controlling our muscles" – such as controlling our speech muscles and refusing to say something that's hurtful, or controlling our muscles to walk away from a situation instead of engaging in conflict. It's helpful to realize what can and can't be controlled in a given situation to help you choose how to react.

The Relationship Between Temper and Environment

We get *angry* when we feel *other people are wrong or have wronged us*. But, we can't control other people or events, so we have to find ways to cope. The tools in this book will help.

If we think *we are wrong*, we worry, feel inadequate and feel worthless. But, after our initial feelings, we can learn to change our thoughts and control impulses, and the tools in this book will teach you how.

When you find yourself getting worked up over a situation, take a deep breath and think about if you are experiencing **angry** or **fearful** temper.

Then think about whether the stress in the situation is a result of the **external environment**—something outside your control—or your **internal environment**, how you are reacting to the situation.

Example: <u>Outer environment triggering angry or fearful temper</u>

- When we feel anxious about a trivial everyday situation that we cannot control and must endure, for example being stuck in traffic, we can **spot angry temper** (frustration at outer environment) and use the **tools** *"If we can't change a situation, we can change our attitude towards it"* and *"We can take secure thoughts"* that it won't last forever and remember that *"Comfort is a want, not a need."*

- The same situation could turn to **fearful temper**, by accusing ourselves with thoughts like, *"I should have left the house earlier," "Why did I take this road?"* and *"I'm always late."* This is a time to remember **tools** like, *"I spot that it is average to get caught in traffic," "This is distressing but not dangerous"* or *"Drop the judgment."*

Example: Inner Environment's reactions to Outer Environment

- Suppose a friend is late picking us up to go to a movie. Initially we may have angry *feelings*. We might have *impulses* to yell at our friend or refuse to go because the movie will have already started by the time we get to the theater. We might have *thoughts* that our friend doesn't care enough about us to be on time or that it's our friend's *fault* that we are so upset. Now we can **spot** our inner feelings of **angry** or **fearful temper** and **use tools** to change our thoughts and control our impulses like *"We can't control the outer environment, we can only control our inner environment's reaction," "Temper is a blindness to the other side of the story," "People do things that annoy us not necessarily to annoy us,"* and *"We excuse rather than accuse ourselves and others"* for the sake of peace.

By using tools, we drop the judgement and change our thoughts and realize that bad traffic or being late to the movies are trivialities, not emergencies. Our friend may have had a flat tire or lost track of time, or traffic may have been slow. Regardless of the reason for the tardiness, we can adjust our plans and still enjoy time together.

> **Calm begets calm, temper begets temper.** – *Angry speech will result in an angry response, speak calmly and things are more likely to cool down.*

BETTER. MENTAL. HEALTH. *for Everyone*

Activity: Applying Tools to Your Situation

To better learn these concepts, reflect on a situation you've experienced involving **outer environment** that caused a temperamental reaction.

Situation: _____

_____

_____

Review the list of tools below and put a check by a few that might help reduce temper in the above situation.

- ☐ We can't control outer environment. We can only control our inner reaction to outer environment.
- ☐ Be self-led, not symptom-led.
- ☐ Symptoms are temporary not permanent.
- ☐ Feelings should be expressed and temper suppressed.
- ☐ We can do the things we fear or hate to do.
- ☐ If we can't decide, any decision will steady us.
- ☐ It's not that we *cannot*, it's that we *care not* to bear the discomfort.
- ☐ Replace an insecure thought with a secure thought.
- ☐ Move our muscles, change our thoughts.
- ☐ Feelings and sensations cannot be controlled, but thoughts and impulses can.
- ☐ There are no uncontrollable impulses, only impulses that are not controlled.
- ☐ Thoughts can be suppressed, dropped or changed.
- ☐ Life is full of frustrations. Frustrations are tolerable and average.

Reading: Temper as a Bridge

Our external environment is everything outside our bodies. Home, parents, friends, school, or work and other people and events make up our external or outer environment.

Our internal environment is everything inside our skin. This internal or inner environment is made up of (1) our internal physical self and (2) our feelings, thoughts, sensations, and impulses.

Our inner environment is far more powerful and alive and more easily disturbed than anything outside us. Yet the everyday irritations of our external environment are what create most of our internal irritations.

Here's an example given by Vanessa of something that happened to her before she participated in this program:

> "I worked hard on an important presentation. I knew my materials well and had prepared my speech. On the day of the meeting, a colleague bumped into me in the hallway spilling my papers to the ground. I got upset because I didn't know if she did it on purpose. I became stressed and uptight. Why did this have to happen today? When I got to the meeting, I was still upset. I was unsure of myself. My stomach felt funny and my palms were sweating. As I rose to begin my presentation, I felt very tense. In spite of all my preparation, I felt insecure."

In this example, the colleague did not just bump Vanessa's body, she also disturbed Vanessa's temper. **Temper is the bridge** over which irritations of the **external environment** can reach across to the **internal environment**. In this case, the "bridge" is not a good thing. It allows a connection that produces undesirable results.

When we are irritated by people or events in our external environment, we can either react with temper or with a sense of humor.

If we react with temper, we will be distracted, upset, or angry. If we react with humor, we will be spared a lot of pain and frustration. Our sense of humor can prevent a bump to our body from spreading to our inner environment and thoughts.

Here's another example Vanessa gave after she had learned how to control her temper and develop a sense of humor:

> "Recently, I was getting lunch at the cafeteria and a woman pushed past me and cut the line. At first, I wanted to push back and tell her to get behind me. Then I remembered the feelings I had when I was bumped on the day of the presentation. I recalled how that made me feel uneasy and tense, and knew my reaction affected me for a long while afterward.
>
> This time, I knew I did not want to get my feelings worked up. I shook my head, smiled and shrugged. It felt much better. Although my temper started to go up, I used my sense of humor and my irritation passed. I excused her—maybe she was in a hurry to eat before a meeting. I was glad I chose to react differently."

Vanessa had learned how to control her temper and develop a sense of humor. She had learned that **temper is our worst enemy and humor is our best friend**.

Reading based on Chapter 8 of *Mental Health Through Will-Training* by Dr. Abraham Low.

Feelings and sensations rise and fall. – *Initial feelings can't be controlled, but if we don't work them up, they will pass.*

" This gave me tools to put events or situations into perspective. "

Gil P., Pittsburgh, PA

BETTER. MENTAL. HEALTH. *for Everyone*

Reading:
Changing Actions and Reactions

When you think of the word temper, do you think about anger, disappointment, unhappy feelings, or tantrums? What do you do when in temper? Do you roll your eyes, ball up your fists, hit or kick something? All these are acts. Each act begins with an intention.

Before we act, we have a goal—something we intend to do. When we carry out the act, we have accomplished our intention.

For example, when we are hungry, we want to eat. Once we have eaten, we have accomplished our intention, which was to eat and not be hungry. After we eat, we feel satisfied. So eating created satisfaction, and we relax.

But, the temperamental act is different. Someone or something angers or annoys us. We intend to stop that irritation, and we have to decide how we will accomplish this. *Our decision* will determine whether our act will be destructive, creative or useful.

If we choose to speak in temper with angry words, then *we are saying that someone has wronged us or someone is wrong*. This intention can't be accomplished because trying to prove to someone that they are wrong is not easy. From the other person's viewpoint, they are not wrong. It is only from our viewpoint that the person is wrong.

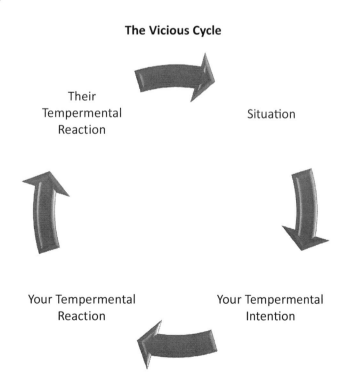

© 2022 Recovery International

What can we do to make them accept our viewpoint? We could yell or shout. That person will probably yell and shout back. It becomes a cruel or vicious cycle that continues.

That's the usual temperamental process. Such outbursts only create casualties or victims. There is no satisfaction. We both become more angry, tired and upset. Each becomes a victim of intentions to prove the other wrong.

To create a satisfactory outcome, **we must change how we react to the situation**, and this takes practice. It is also important to remember that **we can only change our own actions and reactions**—we cannot control how others will act or react.

Reading based on Chapter 40 of *Manage Your Fears, Manage Your Anger* by Dr. Abraham Low.

Endorse for each effort, not just the outcome. – *We congratulate ourselves for each step we take toward well-being or accomplishing a task, even if we didn't succeed.*

BETTER. MENTAL. HEALTH. *for Everyone*

Reading: Sense of Humor

In one of the program sessions, Maria shared an example about the time she missed her stop on the train:

"I was listening to music on my headphones, and I wasn't paying attention. I felt so mad at myself when I looked up and realized the train had passed my stop. I started to work myself up. 'What's wrong with me?' I thought. 'Why am I so stupid?' My stomach started churning, and I felt really heavy.

"Then I remembered to spot my symptoms, and to stop beating myself up and blaming myself for a trivial mistake. I thought about what we learned: *'Don't take yourself so seriously'* and *'Excuse, don't accuse others or yourself.'* I calmed down, got off at the next stop and took another train back to where I needed to be. Before this program, it was easy to blame myself for simple mistakes. I would have stayed upset for the rest of the day. Now I can smile at these mistakes and let them go."

Some people are enemies of themselves. They are fearful and ashamed of their impulses or their actions or their feelings. When people dislike themselves, it is called self-hatred. When people react with a sense of shame or a sense of self-hatred, these reactions are negative judgments against themselves—what we call **fearful temper**. Maria used to be negative about herself and others, but she has learned to smile and even laugh inwardly about trivial mistakes.

People who feel a sense of shame, fear, self-dislike, and self-resentment over daily trivial events have no sense of humor. They take their experiences too seriously.

To feel better about ourselves, we need to develop a sense of good humor. This doesn't mean always cracking a joke or laughing—it might be as simple as smiling at ourselves instead of scowling. How can we do that? Well, we must be trained, and that training must be ongoing.

We must realize that we are human, and we all have a sense of our own importance. But we make the same mistakes everyone else does. We are average. When we ask,

"What's the matter with me?" our answer should be: "Nothing is the matter with me. I am average." Average people don't get worked up over things that are trivial. When we reach that point, we have done two things – we have developed a sense of humor, and we see ourselves as average. When we think of ourselves as average, then we can make mistakes and not be so hard on ourselves.

If we look on our troubles with a great sense of importance, that is the same as having no sense of humor. Self-importance is opposed to a sense of averageness and to a sense of humor. *One way to develop a sense of humor is to get rid of our excessive sense of importance.*

Pay close attention to developing a sense of good humor. We have to give ourselves time and continue the training. We can't be disappointed if we make up our minds today to use our sense of humor and find out tomorrow that we haven't used it. That's perfectly average. We just need to remember to keep working at it.

Reading based on Chapter 17 of *Manage Your Fears, Manage Your Anger* by Dr. Abraham Low.

> **Bear discomfort and comfort will come.** – *Face our fears and worries, we will grow stronger and find more lasting comfort.*

> "
> This has been life changing. I have moved on to heal emotionally, spiritually, and physically since healing mentally with RI training.
> "
> Carolyn B., Charleston, SC

Lesson 2:
Recovery International Language

Objectives:

- Recognize the terms associated with tempermental language.

- Practice using secure language in place of tempermental words.

> I have grown in self-confidence and can handle life very well. My deeper understanding of what affects behavior makes me more tolerant and creates a more secure and relaxed home.
>
> Ron J., Springfield, MO

> This method essentially saved my life by giving me tools to deal with suicidal thoughts. This has benefitted me, my husband, and my son.
>
> Maria O., Miami, FL

Recovery Language and Its Purpose

This program uses language where specific meanings are assigned to certain terms. For more background on why this language is important, see Appendix C. The language serves a number of purposes:

- It is designed so that harmful thoughts can be replaced with helpful ones.
- It helps avoid words that are fearful, judgmental, diagnostic, and that exaggerate events.
- It provides security and reduces triggering phrases.
- It is universal to all participants, helps understanding, and ensures that meetings provide a safe place for everyone.

Temperamental Language: Is *alarming*, *defeating*, or results in *exaggerated*, *negative* or *insecure* descriptions or experiences. These include terms such as:

right	wrong
always	never
can't	idiot
failure	mess
driving me crazy	it's a disaster

Fearful or Angry temper can lead to or be the result of temperamental language. We try to avoid using temperamental language.

Examples:
- Someone makes a comment about something we've said or done, and we say or think, "That person is *always* criticizing me. No matter what I say or do, that person is *never* satisfied." This exaggeration is an example of temperamental language that *leads to angry temper*. Instead, use your "inner smile," and shrug, and think that it's just one person's opinion.

- Someone asks us to do something, and we immediately think, "I *can't* do that. It's *too hard*. If I don't do it *right*, they'll be angry." This is an example of temperamental language that *results from fearful temper*. Instead, look for the first step to get started, or find humor in tackling something new.

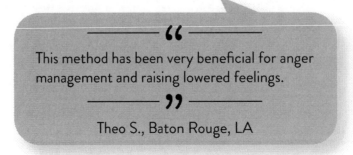

"This method has been very beneficial for anger management and raising lowered feelings."

Theo S., Baton Rouge, LA

Activity: Uncovering Temperamental Language

Reflect on how you describe situations. Write three sentences you have said that use temperamental language (words such as: always, never, right, wrong, and similar terms or phrases).

1. _____

2. _____

3. _____

> **Fearful anticipation is often worse than the realization.** -
> *Worrying about what might happen is often worse than what does happen.*

Secure Language

Secure Language: Is *calming* and *encouraging* and results in *realistic*, *positive* or *secure* descriptions or experiences. Examples of secure language include terms such as:

can	possible
able	try
doable	successful
tolerable	high average

In this program, we learn to identify temper and substitute *secure language* for *temperamental language* in order to **change the way we react to and handle situations**.

Examples:
- Suppose the next-door neighbor is playing their music too loud. If we think "People do things that annoy us, not necessarily to annoy us" then we realize the neighbor probably does not know how loud the music is and is not disturbing us on purpose.

- Suppose we become nervous about going to a party where we don't know many people. We can think "Anticipation is often worse than realization" and remember other times when we've met new people and had a nice time.

We use the secure language of tools to lower temper. Tools are examples of secure, positive language that we use to change our thoughts and drop our temper.

Tools appear throughout this book, and are listed in Appendix A for your convenience. There is no right or wrong in choosing which to apply. Use whatever tools work for you.

For more definitions, see the Glossary of Terms in Appendix B.

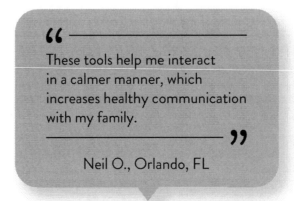

" These tools help me interact in a calmer manner, which increases healthy communication with my family. "

Neil O., Orlando, FL

Activity: Practicing Secure Language

Go back to the previous activity on page 23 and highlight or circle the words or terms that you wrote which are temperamental or negative.

Now, re-write those statements using secure words such as: can, able, possible, or even use "spots" or tools listed on previous pages for the situation you stated.

1. _____

2. _____

3. _____

Every act of self-control leads to a sense of self-respect. –
We feel proud of ourselves when we control our impulses.

Reading: The Purpose of Life is to Maintain Peace

Why do everyday happenings cause so much upset in the world? If events are routine in most cases, our reactions should be routine, too. Events that the average person can deal with should not be upsetting to so many people.

If we feel upset by a routine event, *it is not the event that upsets us but the attitude that we take to the event.*

We can learn to tell the difference between the event that happens and the attitude we take toward it. We have the attitude; the event doesn't. If we allow an event to upset us, it is due to *our* attitude. Although the event cannot be changed, the good news is that **our attitude can be controlled, can be changed, and can be improved**.

For example, we are standing in the checkout line at the store. A woman crowds in front of us. Of course, her actions are rude and inconsiderate, but our attitude will determine whether her action will upset us.

But why should *we* change our attitude toward something or someone that has upset us? That has to do with purpose. Our purpose in life should be to make ourselves and the people close to us—family, friends, neighbors, classmates, or colleagues—feel good. In other words, the purpose of life is to avoid disturbances when possible.

The real aim in life should be to develop a sense of inner peace. What mainly disturbs the peace is **temper**. Temper is opposed to peace. If our purpose is to have peace with others and with ourselves, we must make every effort to reduce our temper.

Temper wants us to be right and others to be wrong. Temper wants to win and have others lose. Temper wants to have power over others. Temper uses power and creates a life of power. When someone is so bent on having power even to the point of beating someone else down, then there will never be peace.

So, while in the checkout line, we can become upset and lose our temper with the woman and her impolite act, or we can take the attitude that the world is full of thoughtless people and ignore her rudeness. We can remind ourselves that **people do things *that* annoy us, not *to* annoy us**, and that if we spend our lives trying to control other people's behavior, we'll never have peace. As we learn how to express ourselves without temper, we will eventually be able to calmly tell the woman where the line is…but if we have temper, it is better to control our speech muscles and not say anything and "excuse, don't accuse."

If we want to maintain peace, we must reduce temper. But that is not easy to do. Temper is a part of our human nature. Temper craves and uses power to destroy peace. We must keep inner peace by controlling temper and by changing our attitudes to disturbances. This program helps us express feelings without temper and have new attitudes about events that happen.

When we learn to control our temper by using these tools, we feel victorious and proud. We gain self-control, self-pride, and self-respect. The more self-respect we feel, the more we are able to reduce our temper. This puts us on the road to maintaining peace and fulfilling the purpose of life. Remember that **every act of self-control leads to a sense of self-respect**.

Reading based on Chapter 19 of *Manage Your Fears, Manage Your Anger* by Dr. Abraham Low.

Face, tolerate and endure discomfort. – *Everyone faces uncomfortable situations, and sometimes we just have to push through it in order to lead a full life.*

Reading: Family and Friends

Think about your own situation. Who irritates you the most – your close relatives and friends or people you don't know as well?

Lesser amounts of irritation come from people we don't know well, such as people at school or work we are not close to or strangers we see in a store. In other words, we tend to be cool toward strangers, but we often lose our temper with people who are close to us. We are more likely to be rude and impatient with family or others close to us than with strangers.

When we are invited to meet up with friends, we are more likely to arrive on time to see who else is there. But if we are expected to be home for dinner, we may arrive late because we think being out with friends is more important than being on time for dinner.

If we are late meeting friends, we may offer an apology or give an excuse for being late. This apology is an expression of service. But we may not even think of apologizing for being late for dinner at home. This lack of courtesy to our family is an expression of domination and personal power.

Indifference to the feelings of others is a form of domination, while concern over how our actions affect others is motivated by service.

If this is our normal behavior, then there is no healthy balance between the motives of service and domination. Domination wins at home, and service wins outside of home. *Too many people save their best behavior for non-family but tend toward domination when dealing with family.*

How can we improve our family life? Learn behaviors and attitudes that express a **healthy balance**, with the spirit of service and cooperation stronger than the spirit of domination.

Reading based on Chapter 4 of *Peace versus Power in the Family* by Dr. Abraham Low.

Lesson 3:
Identifying Trivialities

Objectives:

- Recognize that we are all average people.

- Identify trivial daily events that trigger symptoms.

- Spot the symptoms experienced when worked up.

> "This has given me practical tools to deal with the ups and downs of everyday life."
>
> Marilyn B., Grand Rapids, MI

Averageness

In this program, being average is fine. *Average does not mean mediocre.* Even exceptional people have averageness in their lives. One often hears a celebrity or sports star say: "I'm just an average person at home" or "I put my pants on one leg at a time, just like everyone else."

Averageness helps us understand that:
- Everyone experiences similar trivialities.
- Everyone has temper.
- Everyone gets tense and nervous to a degree.
- Everyone feels urges to lash out in anger or avoid what they fear.
- Our experiences are average.
- Our feelings and sensations are average.

We do not put pressure on ourselves to always react perfectly, no one can. We want to set realistic goals—what we *can* achieve, not what's impossible to achieve. Trying to be exceptional sometimes paralyzes us. Perfection is an illusion. The spot: *Lower your standards and your performance will rise,"* means "relax, and you will do better."

Being average does not have to be dull, either. Average people have wonderful ideas and experiences in their lives, and may excel in a particular task or hobby.

We each have our own average. Some people are early risers and do their best thinking in the morning. That is their average. Others do their best work in the afternoon or late at night. That is their average. We are all good at some things and not so good at others.

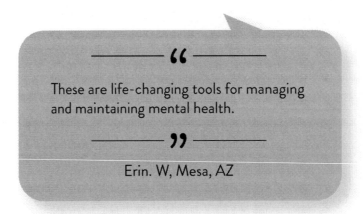

> These are life-changing tools for managing and maintaining mental health.
>
> Erin. W, Mesa, AZ

Activity: Accepting Your Averageness

List at least one thing you feel that you are good at:

_____
_____
_____

List at least one thing you feel that you are not so good at but put in effort:

_____
_____
_____

It's not really how good we are at something that's important. What is important is our effort—that we try to do our best to our own ability, that doing an average job is fine. We try to drop the judgment—of ourselves and of others.

Self-endorsement creates a feeling of security – *Each time we endorse ourselves, we increase our sense of self-control.*

Symptoms

Symptoms are the physical and emotional discomfort we experience right after an upsetting event. Our feelings, sensations, thoughts and impulses are the first signs that we are in temper. The sooner we can spot them, the sooner we can apply the tools to stop from getting worked up further.

These are some average upsetting inner responses we **can't control**:

Feelings	Sensations
Anger	Tenseness
Fear	Tightness (muscles, jaw)
Love	Pressure (head, chest)
Sadness	Adrenaline rush
Excitement	Change in breathing
Jealousy	Pounding heart
Hatred	Wanting to cry
Panic	Sweating
Embarrassment	

Earlier, we reviewed language and terms unique to the RI Method. When referring to symptoms, note that common terms such as "depression, headache, or can't breathe" are not used in the RI Method. Instead, specifically describe what you are experiencing without assigning a diagnosis, such as lowered feelings, pressure in the head, or air hunger.

If you've been diagnosed as having a nervous condition, the sensations you experience following an event may be distressing, but they are not dangerous. This program helps you learn to replace insecure thoughts with secure thoughts to relieve your symptoms.

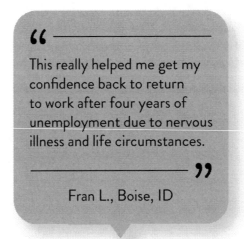

" This really helped me get my confidence back to return to work after four years of unemployment due to nervous illness and life circumstances. "

Fran L., Boise, ID

Trivialities

Trivial events are things that happen in everyday life. They are not right or wrong, they just happen. We give them value with our thoughts, emotions, and actions.

Trivial events may include:
- Obstacles
- Delays
- Inconsiderate people
- Frequent annoyances

Sometimes the small events can get us worked up. When that happens, notice what **physical and emotional changes occur** and **use the tools** in this program to replace the insecure thought with a secure thought. Find a tool to help express feelings without temper.

For instance, technology is wonderful, until it doesn't work! Problems with our computer or cell phone are common, average issues and usually trivial ones in the greater scheme of life. We recognize our jaw is clenched, palms are sweaty, and heart is racing. We could apply the tool **"We can't control the outer environment"** to realize we can't control the computer and this is an average event.

Perhaps we stopped at a coffee shop and the employee got our order wrong. The coffee is expensive and we were looking forward to drinking it. We were in a hurry and didn't have time to go back so they could fix it. We notice we are getting worked up: clenched fists, warm face, and head pressure. We could apply the tool **"We can't change an event, we can only change our attitude toward it"** or **"Excuse don't accuse"** to manage our reaction.

These symptoms are distressing but they are not dangerous. By learning to manage our reactions to small, everyday occurrences, we become more resilient to them. The ability to overcome the small things can help us deal with life's larger issues if and when they occur.

- We can't change an event, we can only change our attitude toward it.
- There is no right or wrong in the trivialities of everyday life.

Activity: Recognizing Trivialities

Write down those every day, trivial events that annoy you. These could be things that occur at home, with friends or family, at work, driving, etc.

Then, list some of the physical and emotional symptoms you experience when that event happens.

Event: _____

    Symptoms: _____

    _____

    Tools: _____

    _____

Event: _____

    Symptoms: _____

    _____

    Tools: _____

    _____

Event: _____

    Symptoms: _____

    _____

    Tools: _____

    _____

Now look at the lists of tools from Lesson 1 or Appendix A, and apply one or two of those to each event you listed. Could any of those help you change your attitude to the event the next time it occurs? Practice applying those tools when the event occurs again and think about if your symptoms are milder once you've used these tools.

Reading: Averageness versus Exceptionality

We can judge an event or ourselves as exceptional, or we can judge an event or ourselves as average.

Why do people want to do the exceptional act, the perfect act? There is no perfection in life. In this program, we stress the importance of being average, of considering a situation average, of wanting to do a job that, on average, is good.

But people don't drop their desire for perfection, for exceptionality. Why not? The reason is simple. We are vain. Everyone is vain. Vanity means we don't want to be like other people. We insist on being better, and stronger, and smarter than other people. Inside, there are powerful impulses that make us want to perform at the highest level.

Every individual craves to be exceptional and superior, to do the perfect job, to be above others and not average. *Everybody hopes to be superior and fears to be inferior.*

To be average means to give up the hope of being superior. People don't like that. They have spent their lifetime dreaming of accomplishing something exceptional. And now we say it's better to give up this habit. That's a big order.

But, it's healthier to take this approach. Otherwise, here is what will happen:

We want to be superior. This means we depend on others to give us credit as being not just average but exceptional, to give us honor, to flatter us. And if we don't get that honor and flattery, we become disappointed because we expected it. Vanity and striving for perfection can be very harmful. Vanity often creates disappointment. This is why we stress the value of averageness.

We don't try to get rid of our vanity. We can never do that. But we can control our vanity, we can *control our impulses to be superior*. And by controlling vanity, it gradually gets weaker and weaker, to the point where we are happy to be average.

Average does not mean mediocre—it means we are like everyone else.

Reading based on Chapter 25 of *Manage Your Fears, Manage Your Anger* by Dr. Abraham Low.

Reading: Don't Sweat the Small Stuff

Most of life is made up of simple everyday happenings - "small stuff." We call these things **trivialities**. We eat, sleep, walk, go to school or work, talk to friends. These actions take up 90 percent or more of our day. Big events such as a wedding, a birth or death in the family, serious illness, or moving from one house to another don't happen very often.

The little events of everyday life create responses in us. Sometimes we don't notice them much, sometimes they make us happy. Sometimes, the responses anger or scare us.

Suppose our best friend doesn't return our phone call or text message immediately. To some this may be trivial, but to others it can lead to frustration, irritation, or anger. The closer the person is to us, the more these little things can irritate, frustrate, or anger us.

We can learn to deal with trivialities without getting upset and acting out in temper. This leads to a more peaceful life.

This training is designed to help us manage our response to trivialities. So what if a person we know walks by and doesn't look at us or speak to us? So what if a stranger stares at us? So what if someone talks too much? That's life. It's no big deal.

We learn to recognize when we are responding to trivial events with anger or fear and then keep from working ourselves up into symptoms or acting out.

Reading based on Chapter 23 of *Manage Your Fears, Manage Your Anger* by Dr. Abraham Low.

Lesson 4: Build Will-Power

Objectives:

- Recognize feelings and impulses and realize that we have a choice in how we react to events.

- Practice strengthening our will-power.

> "RI changed my life for the better and greatly improved my marriage and relationship with others close to me. This method gave me the tools to overcome anxiety, panic attacks and temper, and as a result all my relationships have improved!"
>
> Paul S., Austin, TX

> "I learned I have anxiety and depression, but through this program I have learned to manage it, manage situations, and manage my own expectations."
>
> Linda R., Louisville, KY

Choice

Choice gives us the ability to act, react, or do neither. It allows us to control our thoughts, which can influence the outcome of a situation. Choice is the ability to select spots in our toolkit to take positive action.

When something happens (**an event**), we react with **feelings**. These feelings create an **impulse** to act. We then have a choice of what **action** to take. We can react with calm, anger, or with humor. We can give in to the impulse, or we can apply our new tools to change the outcome.

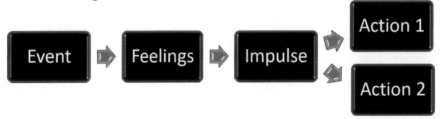

As an example, let's say that Ron came home from work and expected his teenagers to have cleaned their rooms. He saw clothes on the floor, the beds unmade, and dirty dishes on the dressers. His initial feeling was anger at them for not listening or remembering their task. He felt tightness in his jaw and his face getting warm.

The impulse he had was to yell at them and punish them. But Ron knew he had a choice of actions to take. He could apply the tools **"Calm begets calm, temper begets temper."** He could calmly but firmly ask them to pick up their clothes and put the dishes into the sink. Taking the second action helped maintain peace in the family and everyone had a better evening.

These are examples of upsetting initial reactions you **can control**:

Thoughts
"He/She is wrong…to speak to me that way, to ignore me, to boss me around…"

"I am wrong." "The system is wrong."

"The rules are wrong."

"I am worthless." "I will never amount to anything."

Impulses
To speak in anger

To use physical violence

To complain

To run away from discomfort

To stay home and not go (to class, to an event, a gathering)

Activity: Applying the Process of Choice

Now it's your turn to map out a situation that caused you angry or fearful temper.

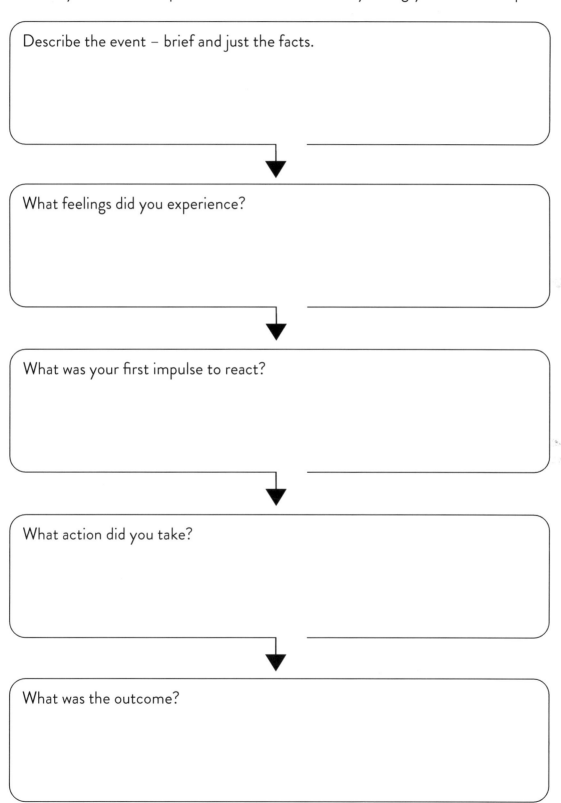

Using Our Will

When we talk about being able to control our outer reactions —what we say and how we act—we refer to our <u>will</u>:
- We can decide which thoughts to think.
- We can decide which words to use.
- We can decide which actions to take.
- We can decide which muscles to command.

By using our tools, we work on developing:
- A determined will.
- The will to effort.
- The will to bear discomfort.
- The will to persevere.
- The will to patience.

Previously we learned that we cannot control our outer environment (events or people), *we can only control ourselves.*

By using our will to control our outer reactions, we can often *influence* the outer environment and others.

For example, when we use the tool **"we choose peace over power"** to drop our temper, our calm reaction can help to calm the reactions of those around us.

The more we practice spotting temper and applying appropriate tools, the more we will be able to control our outer reactions. And the more we do it, the easier it becomes and the better we are at it. Practice, practice, practice.

- We can decide which thoughts to think.
- We can decide which words to use.
- We can decide which actions to take.
- Comfort is a want not a need.
- Life is full of frustrations.
- Frustrations are tolerable.

Will-Power

The tools in this book help us act and think differently than before—if we practice them again and again, then everyday annoyances will not bother us as much. We 'retrain our brain' to respond more calmly to situations. As we do this—**endorse!**—we *congratulate ourselves each time for each little step we take toward controlling angry or anxious thoughts and impulses.*

Dealing with Things INSIDE and OUTSIDE Yourself

1 — Your Will

We have the power to choose:
- How we are going to act
- What we are going to think

2 — Trivialities

Most things that upset us are the routine events in everyday life.

3 — Self-endorsement

We deserve a mental pat on the back for any effort:
- To spot our temper
- To control our thoughts and impulses

Activity: Using Your Will to Change an Outcome

Refer to the previous activity on Applying the Process of Choice (page 39) when you mapped out an event, feelings, impulses, the action you took and the outcome. Below are some tools or spots for coping with everyday occurrences. Indicate a possible outcome of the situation based on using the tools listed.

Tool or Spot	Possible Outcome
Every act of self-control leads to a greater sense of self-respect.	
Feelings and sensations cannot be controlled, but thoughts and impulses can.	
Move our muscles, change our thoughts.	
It's not that we *cannot*, it's that we *care not* to bear the discomfort.	
There are no uncontrollable impulses, only impulses that are not controlled.	

Reading: Choice is the Main Thing

Our *actions* are governed by *impulses* that flow from *feelings* that are caused by an *event*. When things happen outside ourselves, we react with feelings. For example, if somebody we know passes by on the street, it is natural to react first with feelings.

Let's say the person that passed us was a friend, but they didn't say hello. If we are secure, then we'll decide they didn't say hello because they didn't see us. But if we are not secure, if we are over-sensitive, then all kinds of thoughts may crowd into our brain. We may think "My friend disrespected me. They ignored me. They don't like me."

This next step may be either fear or anger. If that person is important, for instance, our boss or somebody that we like, then we might become fearful that they are ignoring us. If they are not that important— an acquaintance or casual friend— then we might get angry. The impulse may then be to challenge them or say something rude. That's an action dictated by anger.

In this way, our actions are governed by impulses that flow from feelings that were aroused by an **event**. A **feeling** is the first thing that happens after an event. That feeling creates an **impulse**. Once the feeling and the impulse have been aroused, we make a judgment, a **decision**. The decision determines whether or not we will act on the feeling and the impulse.

In life everything depends not on feeling, not on impulse, but on the decision—the **choice**—that either releases the impulse or holds it back.

Choice is the main thing in life. And this program teaches us how to think about our impulses, how to choose when to act, what to do or what not to do—*it's our choice*.

Reading based on Chapter 25 of *Manage Your Fears, Manage Your Anger* by Dr. Abraham Low.

Reading: Controlling Impulses

When you think of education, you may think of school. However, our real education to function in this world requires that we train our **impulses**. *We need to learn to hold back expressing feelings such as self-importance, anger, and hatred.* Culture teaches us to hold down many anti-social impulses in our nature.

On some level, everyone feels fear and anger. The fear and anger inside us are always ready to be released as temper.

We are born with temper. Even babies show temper. They don't have to learn how to scream and kick and demand that their needs be met. They do it naturally. When we feel temper, we want to release it right away. *Controlling temper is a matter of culture. It must be learned.*

If we show anger, hatred, or fear, we felt them first on the inside. But, we do not have to show or release them. *We can feel fear or anger and yet keep it inside* until we are able to express your feelings calmly.

We all have feelings, impulses, sensations, and thoughts that are **responses**. But once we release that fear or anger and express it as a threatening gesture or angry words, that's no longer just a response, it becomes an outward reaction of temper.

We must learn to understand and control antisocial thoughts in the everyday frustrations of life, *in order to gain the ability to control our outward reactions.* Once we start spotting and applying the tools, we learn to express feelings without temper. This takes thought and practice.

Reading based on Chapter 31 of *Manage Your Fears, Manage Your Anger* by Dr. Abraham Low.

> **Initial feelings and sensations cannot be controlled, but can be managed.** – *Feelings are natural and spontaneous, but don't attach danger to them or overreact.*

Reading: Using Our Will

Most people have little interest in the will—nor in impulses, beliefs, or controlling muscles. People are much more interested in actions. People think that living means to act.

There are two kinds of actions. One kind of action happens **without our will**, and the other kind of action depends on **what we choose to do**. This second kind of action is decided by our will. That's why it is important to know how the will works.

If we go out and it is raining, the rain has nothing to do with our will. We did not make it rain. It is raining by chance. But we could have checked a weather report and learned that it would rain. Then whether or not we get wet in the rain becomes our choice. We could think ahead by taking an umbrella or a rain coat or we could stay home. Choosing whether or not to take these actions makes getting wet in the rain no longer a chance happening. Getting wet depends on whether or not we exercised our will and planned ahead.

Preparing for something to happen or protecting ourselves against something happening means having the will to be careful. We have to choose between possibilities. So, **will is the same thing as choice**.

Therefore, some of our actions are dictated by chance and others are dictated by choice. An accidental or unforeseen happening is an event that happens by chance. An act of the will happens by intention. To manage our lives well, we need to know the difference:

Act: Chance or Choice?   Choice = Will
       Accident or Intentional?   Intentional = Will

If a dog jumps at us, that can be scary. That's a happening. That is not choice, that is chance. It is not intention; it is accident. It's not will; it's fate. We did not want to become frightened, but we find ourselves in a state of fear. We should know that this was chance and not choice, accident and not intention. *We should not blame ourselves for a chance startle—that is an average reaction.*

We have to do something about a chance event that scares us. We handle our fears by bearing the fear and knowing that being fearful is part of life. We all handle fears. For example, if you see a dog that scares us, we can use our will and move calmly away from the dog or go inside somewhere. However, we must also use our will to *prevent* the fear from turning into a panic that makes us never want to be around a dog again.

To have fear is perfectly average. We are human beings, and we have average fears. But don't work up the fear so that it becomes a panic. An average person can have fears and go ahead and act regardless of the fear.

However, when confronted with a chance event, we must exercise something that is not chance but choice, not accident but **intention**, and this is the **will**.

For example, if your friends try to pressure you to do something, maybe to fight or to insult another student or co-worker, and you worry about what they might say or do if you don't go along with them, you must **exercise your will** and **bear the discomfort** of not giving in to the pressure. Their challenge is fate—it's out of your control—but how you respond is choice, will.

We must have the will to act through our fear and anger as any average person does or is expected to do. *We can bear the discomfort of the fear and anger, and not work them up or give in to them.* If you are able to do that, then you will have accomplished the main principle of this training.

Reading based on Chapter 26 of *Manage Your Fears, Manage Your Anger* by Dr. Abraham Low.

Sensations are distressing but not dangerous. – *Many symptoms of stress are disturbing, but they are not harmful.*

> "This program has put me in more control of my emotions and mood swings."
>
> Dave O., San Diego, CA

Lesson 5:
Practice the Four-Step Method

Objectives:

- Explore the RI Four-Step Method to manage a situation without temper.

- Apply your own example to the Four-Step Method.

> Rather than getting worked up and staying frustrated, I have tools to work myself down. This peace in the inner environment has a bonus of peace in the outer environment. I am easier to get along with. Along with medication and advice of mental health professionals, the RI Method has enabled me to manage bipolar disorder and maintain stability.
>
> Nora A., Oakland, CA

> RI has helped me take back control of my thoughts and emotions. It gave me tools to come back from isolation and rejoin society. It saved my life.
>
> Michael W., Pittsburgh, PA

The Purpose of the Four-Step Example Format

The four-step example is used to help analyze a stressful situation. Giving examples with this format helps us to:

- Report rather than complain.
- Note our symptoms.
- Check our responses.
- Control our behavior.
- Use the tools to change our thoughts.
- See our progress.
- Praise ourselves for our efforts.
- Learn simplicity instead of complexity.

This format was designed so that people learning the method can replicate it at meetings throughout the world. *The format maintains a discipline and structure so that each step is followed concisely and simply with a neutral reporter-like tone.* In a group setting, or when participating in online or telephone meetings, we learn by listening to others and then practice by volunteering to read, spot or give examples.

> **Feelings are not facts.** – *We may feel guilty or hopeless, but that doesn't mean we are guilty or have no hope.*

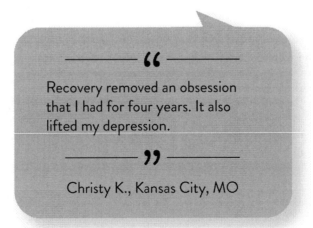

> "Recovery removed an obsession that I had for four years. It also lifted my depression."
>
> Christy K., Kansas City, MO

The Four-Step Method

The four-step example is the core of this program and of every RI support meeting. This outline describes the steps, followed by a more detailed description and a worksheet. Extra example worksheets are included in the back of the workbook in Appendix C.

Part 1: Event
Report a single situation or event that occurred—an everyday event when you began to work yourself up. Focus on a brief description of what happened: specifically, what triggered temper and symptoms?

Part 2: Symptoms
Report the symptoms you experienced-both physical and mental. *(For instance, angry and fearful thoughts, confusion, palpitations, disturbing impulses, tightness in your chest, lowered feelings, sweaty palms, and so on.)*

Part 3: Spotting
Report your spotting of fearful and angry temper, the Recovery International tools you used to help yourself, and your self-endorsement for your effort.

Part 4: Outcome
Begin with "Before I had my Recovery training," and describe the temperamental reaction and symptoms you would have experienced in former days. What would have happened then versus what happened now? (This will help you to note the progress you have made.)

Endorse yourself for your effort or any improvement!

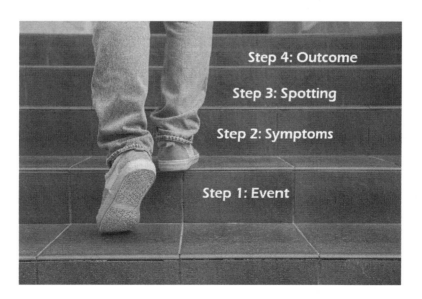

Sample Four-Step Example

The way we practice using the tools and learn better habits is by giving examples following the four steps:

Part 1: Event – Briefly describe an incident.
I went to the parking lot to go home and found that I had left my lights on and my car battery was dead. That's when I began to get worked up.

Part 2: Symptoms – Describe your symptoms: Feelings, impulses, sensations, thoughts.
I felt angry, my heart started racing, I wanted to cry, I thought, "How could I be so stupid?"

Part 3: Spotting – What tools did you use? How did you endorse yourself?
I noted that this is an average, common mistake. These symptoms were distressing but not dangerous. I decided, planned and acted by calling roadside assistance, then calling my husband to let him know I would be home late. I endorsed myself for remembering to use these tools.

Part 4: Outcome – What would have happened before your RI training?
Before RI, I would have stomped around, yelled a bunch of swear words, kicked something, called my husband in tears, and let it ruin my whole evening by berating myself repeatedly. Instead, I congratulated myself for taking care of it without overreacting.

We have practiced some of these steps already in earlier parts of the workbook. With more practice in this section, you will be able to put together your own examples and use a variety of tools.

Activity: Deconstructing a Four-Step Example

Read the following example and then pull out the phrases or sentences for each of the four steps.

"I drove into the gas station, and another car came to the same pump from the opposite direction. He waved his fist at me—obviously thinking he had the right of way. This is when I began to work myself up. I got angry, confused, I felt like crying—I thought, 'Who does he think he is…?' Then I started spotting that I could not control his actions, though he was doing something that irritated me. It was a triviality—not important in the grand scheme of things. I could control my inner environment, and excuse rather than accuse. I endorsed for this effort and waved him in as I drove to another pump. As I was pumping gas, I found myself smiling at how I would have reacted before my training—I would have either said something nasty to him or berated myself for being a wimp. I would have stayed angry all the way home and griped about it to my family. It would have been a vicious cycle of fear and anger. Instead, I could shrug it off and go on to have a nice evening."

Part 1: Event
Use a highlighter or underline the portion of the example that describes the event.

Part 2: Symptoms
Circle the symptoms she was experiencing.

Part 3: Spotting
Highlight the tools or spots she used to change her thoughts. Did she endorse?

____ Yes   ____ No

Part 4:
What would have happened before her RI training?

_____

_____

Activity: Constructing Your Own Example

Think of a recent trivial event that got you worked up. Use the outline below to construct your example in the style of the Four-Step Method.

Part 1: Event
Report a single situation or event that occurred - an everyday event when you began to work yourself up. Focus on a brief description of what happened: specifically, what triggered temper and symptoms? Indicate that you have finished this step by writing: "That's when I began to get worked up…"

Your Example:

_____

_____

_____

_____

Part 2: Symptoms
Report the symptoms you experienced-both physical and mental. (For instance, angry and fearful thoughts, confusion, palpitations, disturbing impulses, tightness in your chest, lowered feelings, sweaty palms, and so on.) These are some average upsetting inner responses you **can't control**.

<u>Feelings</u>	<u>Sensations</u>
Anger	Tenseness
Fear	Tightness (muscles, jaw)
Love	Pressure (head, chest)
Sadness	Adrenaline rush
Jealousy	Change in breathing
Hatred	Pounding heart
Panic	Wanting to cry
Embarrassment	Sweating

These are examples of upsetting initial reactions you **can control**.

Thoughts

"They are wrong to speak to me that way, to ignore me, to boss me around…"
"I am wrong." "The system is wrong." "The rules are wrong."
"If I don't let off steam, I will burst." "I will get sick."
"I am worthless." "I will never amount to anything."

Impulses

To speak in anger
To use physical violence
To complain
To run away from discomfort
To stay home and not go (to class, to an event, a gathering)

What were your symptoms?

_____

_____

_____

Part 3: Spotting and Endorsement

Report your spotting of fearful and angry temper, the Recovery International tools you used to help yourself, and your self-endorsement for your effort. Look at the diagrams of Temper and Environment in Lesson 1, pages 8 and 11, and describe which you experienced: Angry or Fearful Temper; Internal or External Environment.

_____

_____

_____

Look at the lists of tools throughout the workbook and in Appendix A and describe which could be used to manage the reaction to this incident.

_____

_____

_____

_____

What self-endorsement applies in this example?

_____

_____

_____

Part 4: Outcome
Describe what would have happened *before the training*—the reaction and discomfort you would have experienced in former days:

_____

_____

_____

_____

Describe your reaction *after using the tools* in this workbook:

_____

_____

_____

Endorse yourself for your effort or any improvement!

Note: In an RI support meeting, after each example is presented, other group members "spot" on that example by identifying other tools that they noticed were used or could have been used. The example giver is not allowed to speak during this portion, only listen.

BETTER. MENTAL. HEALTH. *for Everyone*

Reading: Using Humor to Control Temper

We all make bad decisions at times and behave in ways that don't make us proud. But we soon learn that acting out, throwing tantrums, and exploding when we are angry is not in our own best interest.

If we have an outburst of temper and can see right away that the explosion is silly and laugh it off, then we are much less likely to have another temperamental outburst the next time we feel angry. Laughing it off relaxes us and gives us a way to defuse annoying incidents.

Here are some examples from Juan and Will, who went through this program.

> *Juan*: "People used to say I had a bad temper. It was hard to get along with others, even my friends and especially my parents. I would always tell people off. I was loud and it made me feel important. But it was exhausting, I couldn't sleep and I didn't do well in school."

> *Will*: "I have always been angry, too. When I was little, if things didn't go my way, I would lash out by hitting myself on the head. I would kick a wall or anything else that was in my way. I was hurting myself. I behaved this way all through school. I was miserable. I see now I had angry feelings and fearful temper. I started asking myself: What was I afraid of? Why was I so self-destructive? What caused my anger to explode?"

Before Juan and Will went through this training, they approached everything in a temperamental way and they always felt stressed, angry, fearful, and unsettled.

> *Juan*: "Just the other day, I saw a friend at the store. I said 'hey' to him, but he just ignored me. I spoke to him again, and he said, 'Can't you see I'm listening to my music?' Then he turned away to look at something. I was mad and said something very rude to him, but he didn't hear me, and I walked away.

> Once I thought it through, though, I was able to laugh about him being so oblivious and wrapped up in his music. If this same thing had happened a year ago, I would have told him off and insulted him some more. That would have been the end of the friendship.

© 2022 Recovery International

Thanks to this program, I know that my actions were from my temper. Now I see that I acted out because I was angry and afraid, but controlling my anger gives me a sense of accomplishment."

Juan used to live in constant temper. But now he has dropped his feeling of self-importance and developed a sense of humor. Because of this, irritations from the external environment hardly affect his internal environment.

Will: "I got a new job, but I didn't like it. I thought it was a boring. I felt like quitting. One day I was in one of my angry moods, so I skipped work. Afterwards, I thought I would lose my job. I knew I needed to call my boss, but I was afraid. Then I remembered hearing that if you fear something, the thing you really fear is feeling humiliated or uncomfortable. What you need to do is **face your fear**. You need to *do what you fear to do and tolerate the discomfort*.

I finally got up the nerve and called my boss. He just asked me to come back as soon as I could. What a relief! After that, I began to face my fears and not avoid them."

Will had been struggling with his temperamental ways since childhood. But he has learned to control his angry and fearful temper.

There are times when one of them slips back into their old ways—setbacks do happen. By continuing to practice this system of self-discipline, we learn that *temper is the result of an inner arrogance that sets itself up to judge who is right and who is wrong.*

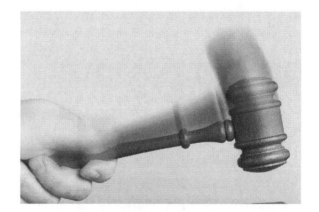

This arrogance is due to the sense of our own vanity and self-importance and cannot be overcome unless we develop a sense of humor. **A sense of humor will help us gain humility, and help us control our internal environment.**

Reading based on Chapter 8 of *Mental Health Through Will-Training* by Dr. Abraham Low.

Lesson 6:
Spot the Key Concepts

Objectives:

- Practice spotting temper, muscle control and muscle movement.

- Learn to identify sabotage.

> "
> Recovery helped me continue on with my life after I developed psychosis at age 25. With the help of this program, I returned to school, earned graduate degrees, and I got married.
> "
>
> Matthew M., Hartford, CT

> "
> Our Recovery training saved our marriage as we used the tools we learned, and we taught them to our children, too. Though we went through some very hard times, we found that by learning to deal with trivialities you are better able to deal with the bigger issues of life.
> "
>
> Alexa R., Davenport, IA

What is Sabotage?

Sabotage is:
- When we ignore or choose not to practice what we have learned.
- When we do not do what is best for our mental health.

Examples of sabotage include:
- Using temperamental language.
- Avoiding the use of the "spots" or "tools."
- Self-diagnosing.
- Using the *judgment* of right and wrong in everyday, trivial events.
- Not controlling muscles—whether to stop what we don't want to do or start what we need to do.
- Failure to endorse yourself.

We must learn to be aware of when we are sabotaging our efforts. We sabotage when we don't use the tools to change our thoughts and control our impulses. We sabotage when we participate in temperamental deadlocks or vicious cycles because of unresolved fearful or angry temper.

As we become more aware of what we do to sabotage ourselves, we can spot more quickly instances of potential sabotage and use the tools to redirect our thoughts and impulses. The more familiar we become with using the tools and the more we practice using them to handle daily trivialities, the less we will engage in sabotage.

Expectations can lead to disappointments. – *Keep expectations realistic.*

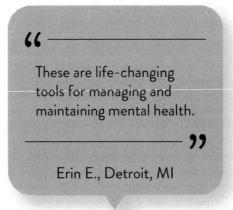

> These are life-changing tools for managing and maintaining mental health.
>
> Erin E., Detroit, MI

Activity: Overcoming Sabotage

Write about a time when you were *not* able to drop your temper.

_____

_____

Circle some tools that could have been used in this instance:

Some Tools for Temperamental Language

Be group-minded not self-minded.

Drop the judgment.

There is no right or wrong in the trivialities of daily life.

We control our speech muscles.

Feelings are not facts, they can lie to us.

Feelings and sensations cannot be controlled, but thoughts and impulses can.

Feelings call for expression, temper for suppression.

Objectivity can wipe out emotionalism.

We excuse rather than accuse ourselves and others.

Outer environment can be rude, crude and indifferent.

We endorse rather than indict ourselves and others.

We drop the ambition of wanting to be perfect.

A sense of averageness brings balance.

Every act of self-control brings a greater sense of self-respect.

We strive for peace, order and calm.

Tempers are frequently uncontrolled, not uncontrollable.

Temper is intellectual blindness to the other side of the story.

If you used one of these tools, would the outcome have been better? What might have happened instead?

_____

_____

Review of Key Concepts

This is a review of the most important elements that are found in each example. After spotting on each example, work through these to reinforce your learning and further reduce symptoms.

1. **Angry Temper** - negative judgments (resentment, impatience, indignation, disgust, hatred) directed against another person or situation.

2. **Fearful Temper** - negative judgments (discouragement, preoccupation, embarrassment, worry, hopelessness, despair, sense of shame, feelings of inadequacy) directed against oneself.

3. **Muscle Control** - controlling the impulse to do something that would be bad for our mental health (Example: not controlling our speech muscles).

4. **Muscle Movement** - commanding the muscles to do something that we are resistant to do (Example: attending a meeting when we'd rather stay home).

5. **Sabotage** - when we ignore or choose not to practice what we have learned in this program. When we do not do what is best for our mental health. (Example: not endorsing).

(Note: In a peer group meeting, there is sometimes a recap of these concepts. The Example Giver does not participate in this review—they listen to what others are saying.)

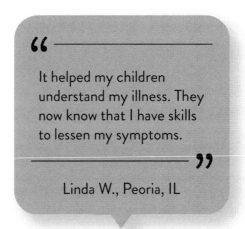

" It helped my children understand my illness. They now know that I have skills to lessen my symptoms. "

Linda W., Peoria, IL

Activity: Concept Review

Choose the example written up in Lesson 5 and write down each of these elements that apply:

1. **Angry Temper** – Did you have negative judgments against another person?

   _____

   _____

2. **Fearful Temper** – Did you have negative judgments directed against yourself?

   _____

   _____

3. **Muscle Control** – Did you control an impulse to do something that would have been bad for your mental health?

   _____

   _____

4. **Muscle Movement** – Did you command your muscles to do something that you were resistant to do?

   _____

   _____

5. **Sabotage** – What did you ignore or not practice? (Did you remember to endorse?)

   _____

   _____

> **Temper is blindness to the other side of the story.** – *Temper prevents you from seeing the other person's point of view.*

Reading:
Three Stages of Temper and the Inner Smile

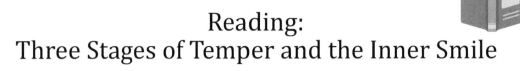

Carl gave this example in a group session:

> "One afternoon I was watching a movie on TV, and my brother and his friend walked in. My brother's friend said that the movie I was watching was stupid. I started to become irritated because it was a movie that I really liked. He kept on saying how stupid the movie was and why, and I got more and more angry. I wanted to yell at him and tell him that he was the one that was stupid.
>
> Then I remembered I could use the tools I had learned. I spotted my temper and decided not to answer. I gave myself time to cool down. I thought about the inner smile and knew it was ridiculous to let my temper rise and take control of my actions. I reminded myself not to take myself too seriously. I just ignored him and kept watching, and he and my brother got bored and went into the other room and left me alone.

> Before I learned this method, I would have yelled at my brother's friend, and he would have laughed and teased me some more. I would have gotten more upset and stomped out of the room and not gotten to finish watching the movie. I would have continued to be angry for the rest of the afternoon."

What Carl was talking about when he described how he became irritated at his brother's friend is the *flare* phase of temper. If we spot the flare, as Carl did, then we can immediately hold it down. We've learned that temper is natural. We all have it. However, what we must do is to prevent the immediate flare phase of temper from becoming expressed temper.

If Carl had confronted his brother's friend during this phase and spoken angry words in a nasty tone of voice, that would have been an immediate temperamental reaction. That would have started a chain reaction with his brother's friend yelling back and Carl striking out at him.

Next, Carl would have passed into the after-effect of his temperamental experience. Even after he left the room, the inner effect would still have been there for him as he dwelled on how stupid his brother's friend was. He could have been angry for hours, for days, or even weeks. This silent after-effect is the most dangerous part of the temperamental cycle.

Again, the temperamental cycle begins with a **flare**, then passes to an **immediate reaction**, and then to the **after-effect**. After the angry words, the after-effect gradually sinks down to the level where no words are spoken but thoughts continue to form inside.

Flaring up of temper is unavoidable when we are angry and irritated. We have to work on training ourselves to spot flare ups so that they do not become immediate spoken reactions. *We must learn to hold temper down and not give it expression.*

How is that done? How can you hold down temper even if it is in the flare stage? Because of his training, Carl was able to spot his temper immediately. He knew in a second that it was ridiculous to let temper rise and express itself over something so trivial.

We call this thought that something is ridiculous the *'inner smile'*. The inner smile cannot be seen on the outside, and the laugh is not expressed as a sound or as a spoken joke. It is simply an inner reaction in which you feel or say to yourself, "This is ridiculous." We must keep the inner smile in our mind and plant the thought in our brain, "This temper is ridiculous." When we think something is ridiculous, then we cannot take it seriously.

Once we feel anger and express it, we are being overly serious about the insult that we've suffered. If we don't take our reaction seriously, then it can't produce further temper. So, if we spot a flare of temper as being ridiculous, we can get rid of it. If we constantly express fear, anger, worry, or embarrassment it means that we take ourselves too seriously. Our training teaches that temper is childish. When we learn to spot it and we ridicule it, then we don't take it seriously and it disappears.

The flare up of temper is unavoidable. It is our nature that the moment we feel provoked, our temper flares. And we can't get rid of our nature. However, we can **control our reaction** to the flare, and the actions or speech that follows.

During the incident with his brother's friend, it was natural for Carl's temper to flare in response to the teasing about the movie. However, he was able to use the inner smile and counteract the temper flare.

We can learn to do that, too. It will take practice, however, the reward will be great. Because he used his inner smile, Carl avoided an unpleasant reaction and its after-effect of inner upset. He was able to watch the rest of the movie in peace and enjoyment.

The next step, after learning to control a temperamental response, is to learn to express ourselves calmly and without temper. This, too, takes practice over time.

Reading based on Chapter 47 of *Manage Your Fears, Manage Your Anger* by Dr. Abraham Low.

Reading: Impulse Control

Everything we do starts with an impulse that tells us to do it. We have the impulse to read a book. After reading the book for a while, we get the impulse to go outside. We may or may not follow the impulse. But, if we do go outside, we do so because our impulse suggested it.

After feeling an impulse, we engage in a thought process called the *preview*. After feeling the desire or impulse to read the book, we ask ourselves, "Should I read the book? Is this the right thing to do at this time? Are there other things I should be doing?" After we read the book, we ask ourselves, "Was it right for me to read the book? Am I glad I did it?" That is what we call the *review*.

After an impulse, every action is preceded by a preview and followed by a review. Usually, we don't realize we are doing this, it happens automatically.

We must learn to spot our preview and our review. These are not always obvious. Both the preview and the review can be either wrong or hurtful, or right and beneficial.

Also, because all actions start with an impulse, it is important to know what impulses are. *An impulse produces an action that will either hurt you or benefit you.* The same impulse may also hurt or benefit others. So, there are *two* relationships that we have to spot. One is the relationship to our own well-being, and the second is the relationship to the well-being of others.

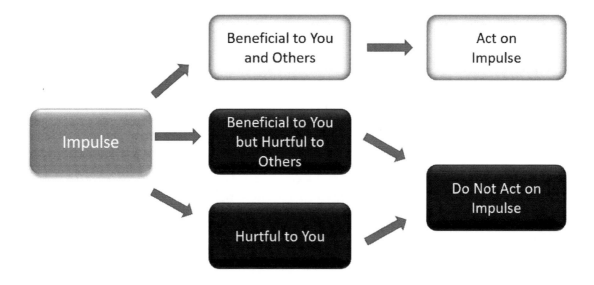

If the preview we form is that an impulse is likely to harm us, then we must control it and not act on it. If the preview we form is that the impulse is not likely to harm us, then we might not have to control it. But we can't only think of ourselves. We must consider others, too. If our impulse is likely to harm others, we must control it. If the impulse is likely to benefit others, then it is safe to release it.

It is difficult to preview and review impulses. When we allow ourselves an outburst of temper, we actually feel a sense of relief afterwards. We got something off our chest. But this relief only lasts for a moment. If others are present, they may answer in temper or laugh at us. Then, the only way to get the feeling of relief back is to have another temperamental outburst. This can go on for hours, even days—with constant attacks and counter-attacks. It becomes a temperamental deadlock, with no one winning.

How can we prevent deadlocks and achieve a win-win situation? Learn to preview and review our impulses. *Do not act on impulses that will harm ourselves or others.*

Reading based on Chapter 27 of *Manage Your Fears, Manage Your Anger* by Dr. Abraham Low.

Lesson 7:
More Key Concepts

Objectives:

- Explore how accepting some discomfort helps to overcome fears.

- Recognize the difference between fellowship and sovereignty.

> "Before Recovery, I felt helpless. But now, my relationship with my family has become peaceful and friendly. They have a better understanding of mental illness and ways to help me cope."
>
> Kathy C., Orlando, FL

> "It's been very helpful for me to deal with my anxiety and depression. Since using this method, I've only had a few major panic attacks. My father and mother noticed the change in me also and I get along much better with them."
>
> Ron Z., Chicago, IL

Comfort and Discomfort

In this program we learn that *comfort is a want, not a need*. We can experience discomfort such as tenseness when we are confronted with something stressful. And it is normal to want relief, but we need to learn to *bear the discomfort*. Practicing this method will bring relief as we build new habits.

Symptoms that are caused by tenseness or fearful or angry temper are average reactions, they are distressing but not dangerous. Once we recognize this, then we are able to *command our muscles* to act against the symptoms and we begin to relax. The result is that we have comfort.

We will never be rid of all discomfort. Fear and tension are a part of normal life. However, we can reduce symptoms to an average or normal level by being willing to bear the discomfort. If we use our will to take positive action despite our fear or anger, then peace and comfort will come.

Example: We are faced with doing something new for the first time, like attending a group meeting, and we are experiencing some fearful temper because we will be with people we don't know, which causes discomfort. However, by using our will, moving our muscles and bearing the discomfort, we realize that there is no danger in this discomfort. We go to the meeting and give ourselves a big reason to endorse for the effort we've made. And as we continue to attend meetings, comfort comes.

Comfort is a want, not a need. – *Learning to accept discomfort is key to self-management.*

Self-Focused vs. Group-Minded

Sovereignty: is selfishness, self-focused, self-centered.

Fellowship: is group-mindedness—putting the interest of the group above your own personal interests.

We distinguish between sovereignty (self-focused) and fellowship (group-minded) in order to achieve peace and health in our daily lives. When you are by yourself at home, you can do what you want and dress however you wish. You can be self-focused. However, we are often in situations where we have to consider others and must be group-oriented.

Fellowship is shifting our focus from our individual rights to our responsibility to the group. In most groups, we should not try to dominate situations or people around us. Instead, we should strive to work towards being more group-minded by thinking about what is best for the group (family, friends, co-workers, public places) and act on that basis.

Remember, though, that we cannot keep others from being selfish or from seeking to dominate us—we cannot control the outer environment.

However, we can:
- Spot (silently) sovereignty/selfishness in others and then keep ourselves from over-reacting to it (working ourselves up).
- Suggest (if it is safe and appropriate to do so) a more group-minded approach that will benefit everyone.

Can you think of some instances of people being self-minded when it was more appropriate to be group-minded?

_____

_____

What tools could be used to keep from getting "worked up" in those situations? (Refer to Appendix A)

_____

_____

Be group-minded, not self-minded. - *We need good relationships. Selfish behavior undermines them.*

Activity: Belonging to a Group

List those groups that you are part of: family, school, community, work, clubs, organizations, hobbies, etc.

_____   _____

_____   _____

_____   _____

_____   _____

Of those groups on your list, choose one or two and reflect on how your behavior and thinking changes when you are in that group.

Group: _____

When I'm with this group, I act/do/think ….

_____

_____

_____

_____

_____

_____

_____

Reading: Service and Fellowship

Robert gave this example in a group session:

> "The other night, my girlfriend Jessica was walking with her friend. I was on my way to the store to buy bread for my mother. I asked Jessica to come with me to the store, but she told me that she was going to walk her friend home. I stormed off before she could finish. After I left them, I was pretty angry, but then I spotted that Jessica wasn't wrong and I shouldn't expect to control her. Pretty soon I stopped feeling angry.
>
> Before this program, I would have stayed furious at Jessica for not doing what I asked her to do, but this time I decided to drop my temper. We saw each other later and I didn't even bring up what had happened.
>
> In the past, we had constant fights because neither of us would give in, and I would stay angry for a long time. Now I spot my urge to dominate, and we argue much less. I feel proud of that change."

In Robert's example, he was running an errand, he ran into Jessica, and he expected her to drop what she was doing and go with him. He got angry. All the upset was caused by a simple errand. It would appear to be a fight about nothing. Why do people fight over 'nothing'?

Any fight is centered around a *purpose* and rooted in a *motive*. For Robert, the purpose was to go to the store for his mother. But what was the motive? A willingness to help his mother was the motive that made Robert head out to the store in the first place.

The original motive—to run an errand for his mother—was **service**. *Service aims to achieve the goal of peace.* It creates good will and promotes the well-being of the group. This motive of service and group welfare was suddenly dropped after Jessica appeared. The new motive became competition and domination. What prompted that change in attitude?

When we are alone at home, we may do as we please as long as we do not hurt ourselves or others. We are **sovereign**. *Sovereignty here means domination, unrestricted power, and no concern for the rights, needs, or wishes of others.*

That sovereignty gets limited the moment others are in the room or we step out into the street. Now we are subject to rules that limit our rights and our behavior. When we are with other people, we are a member of a group.

In a group, the members have equal rights. This is called **fellowship**, which is the opposite of sovereignty. *Fellowship means service, self-control, and respect for the rights of others.*

Groups may be loosely connected, like a crowd in the street, or close-knit, like a family. All kinds of groups exist with different degrees of fellowship. A group of friends should have far more fellowship than a group of students in a class at school, and the group of students in a class at school should have more fellowship than a group of strangers at a town meeting.

The more closely a group is linked, the more it should be filled with the spirit of fellowship. In a family, fellowship ought to be at its maximum, sovereignty at its minimum. But obviously that is not so, because temper is standard in many families. The same is true with boyfriends and girlfriends.

When Robert agreed to go to the store for his mother, his motive was to be helpful. Perhaps Robert did not really want to go to the store for his mother, so his agreeing to run the errand may have been a polite gesture and not a true wish for fellowship. But *in group life, an insincere or fake gesture of fellowship is far more valuable than a sincere expression of sovereignty or selfishness.*

With Jessica, Robert's motive was different. He and Jessica were often in a state of temperamental deadlock. So, when Robert asked Jessica to go with him to the store, it was based on his desire to get her to do what he wanted. His temperamental outburst was sincere. But sincerity of this kind is not a positive.

In this program, we often speak of symbols and symbolic victories. One of the most damaging symbols is the desire for sovereignty. Robert imagined that he ruled in his dealings with Jessica. The result was that their relationship was often turned into a battlefield.

However, because of what he has learned, Robert is beginning to see that the idea of sovereignty is an empty, childish symbol, and fellowship is a mature and proud achievement.

Reading based on Chapter 3 of *Mental Health Through Will Training* by Dr. Abraham Low.

We can break old habit patterns. – *Changing habits takes practice; keep trying and change will come.*

Reading: Behavior Motives: Service or Domination

Do you ever wonder why we do certain things or act a certain way? *Behavior is guided by motives. There are two kinds of motives: service and domination.*

The motive of **service** produces love, friendship, neighborliness, loyalty, honesty, and courtesy. The motive of **domination** produces anger, hatred, disagreement, jealousy, envy, and discourtesy.

These two motives do not exist alone in their pure states. Most of us have both motives within us. We may want to be of service, but there is also a part of us that wants to dominate.

How can a person manage both motives of behavior? The way to do this is to develop a healthy balance, especially within a group.

We all know people who insist on dominating a group. These people always want to have it their way. They are not open to give and take. They have an attitude of "it's my way or the highway" or "if I can't have my way, I'm out." They turn group life into an endless struggle. On the other hand, a person motivated only by service and doing what others want can become boring and irritating.

Have you ever played the game "tug of war"? In this game, one group pulls a rope in one direction, and another group pulls the rope in the opposite direction. Suppose the pulling strength of the two groups is equally balanced. There will be no action, and both groups will end up standing where they start. On the other hand, if the groups are too unequal, there will be no contest. The stronger group will have a blow-out victory over the weaker group. The only way to have an interesting contest is if the pulling power of one team just overbalances the power of the other team.

So it is with motives. The system works better if the opposing forces are neither equally matched nor too unequally matched. **We maintain a healthy state if the motive of service just over-balances domination without overpowering it.**

Reading based on Chapter 4 of *Peace versus Power in the Family* by Dr. Abraham Low.

Reading: Frustration is Common

We all have **frustrations** and disappointments on a daily basis. We often feel dissatisfied with what we do and say. We sometimes feel that we, or others, can do better. Many people are not satisfied with their work, with their conduct or their accomplishments.

Since everyone is frustrated at some point in life, frustration is average. Not only is frustration average, but it is common throughout our lives.

What we practice doing is holding down the frustrations to a low level so that they do not overwhelm us. There is a simple way to hold down frustrations: *"When we deal with everyday life, with routine happenings, don't believe that they are emergencies."*

Real emergencies happen very rarely in life. Nevertheless, we can have big disappointments from trivial events. Little things that turn into big frustrations are common—the TV doesn't work, our friend is late coming over, or someone talks about us behind our backs. These events should not cause us to be severely disturbed. With practice, we learn to apply tools and not work it up.

If we think of every event as an emergency, then we work ourselves up, and become angry and anxious. Frustrations and disappointments can become too much to bear. We must understand that frustration is average and happens all the time. We become miserable if we treat frustrations and disappointments as emergencies. It is important to change the belief that life is full of emergencies. *Frustrations can be tolerated and are average.*

Reading based on Chapter 9 of *Manage Your Fears, Manage Your Anger* by Dr. Abraham Low.

> "This made me stable, contented and happy. That benefits my loved ones by making me present to them."
>
> Tony G., Boulder, CO

Lesson 8: Join a Peer-led Meeting

Objectives:

- Prepare to join a Recovery International peer-led meeting and learn the different formats of meetings that are available.

- Understand the meeting agenda and guidelines that participants follow.

- Become familiar with the role of the peer leader in meetings.

> I have a much better understanding of the problems and needs of people with mental health issues. For me personally, it has helped me understand myself better and makes me a better person who can help to others.
>
> Mark S., Naperville, IL

> I use these tools every day. Without RI, I could not be a happy, successful, productive person. I was very low-functioning before I found Recovery and now I can live an average life.
>
> Eleanor L., Duluth, MN

Support Group Meetings

In addition to this workbook and other publications, Recovery International offers several ways to participate in support group meetings to practice giving examples and using your tools. To find a meeting near you, see schedules of the various types of meetings, or download a Newcomer Packet visit our website: recoveryinternational.org.

Community Meetings: In-person meetings are held in communities throughout the country. They are run by trained peer leaders who assist in learning how to spot and give examples. Affiliate organizations also offer meetings abroad.

Telephone Meetings: Telephone meetings are available at various times daily. Intro to the RI Method training sessions and Literature meetings are available at no cost. Other telephone meetings require membership to attend.

Online Meetings: Online meetings offer the benefit of attending from your own home, and allow for interaction with the leader and other participants through screen sharing of readings and spots. An online welcome meeting is a good place for beginners to start.

Chat Meetings: Chat meetings enable you to post examples and spot on others' examples in real time through moderated yet informal chat format postings.

Facebook Meetings Page: This private group allows people to post examples and spot on others' examples 24/7 in a moderated setting. To send a request to join the group, go to Facebook and search "Recovery International Meeting Page."

Note that membership is required for some of our telephone and online meetings. Membership is encouraged for all participants so that you will receive weekly e-mails and quarterly newsletters to enhance and support your experience.

You can find more information and meeting schedules on our website at recoveryinternational.org. We invite you to seek out a group meeting near you, or consider Leader Training to open a meeting in your community!

Meeting Structure

Our peer leaders are volunteers—they are average people who have been through what you are going through. They have practiced the method for many years, and were mentored and trained in the procedures of running a meeting and leading examples. In these ways, they are an invaluable resource to all meeting participants.

The meetings are 60-90 minutes long, highly structured for effectiveness, and follow a similar outline no matter the meeting format or location:

- Welcome
- Introductions & Announcements
- Selected Reading from one of Dr. Low's books
- Examples from Participants and Spotting (majority of the meeting time)
- Voluntary Contributions
- Questions and Comments
- Mutual Aid & Social Time

Newcomers are encouraged to watch a short video on the Example period of the meeting on the website.

Anti-social responses must not be expressed. – *Don't act on thoughts or impulses that are not group-minded or may harm others.*

> "I think the writings of Dr. Low have shown me a reliable method for confronting my own struggles with mental illness. It gives me concrete steps to cope."
>
> Sam H., Santa Fe, NM

Meeting Guidelines

This is what to expect when you attend a meeting—whether in the community, online or by phone:

- We learn to report, not complain; and to describe, not interpret. We don't try to convince. We don't dramatize.
- During the giving of example, the group doesn't speak. During the comments, the example giver doesn't speak.
- If you wish to comment on the example, raise your hand. (Telephone training will teach alternate protocols.)
- In a small group, the leader may go around the table and ask each person to comment. If you are called on, but do not wish to comment, simply say "pass."
- The comments from the group are to be directed in the third person to the example leader, not to the person who gave the example.
- We do not bring our own experience into someone else's example. We comment on their example only, not how we would handle it, or if we had done something similar.
- The examples are about trivial events of everyday life. We do not deal with major life incidents or traumatic events, but learning how to manage daily challenges will make managing larger matters easier.
- Be brief: details and descriptions are kept to a minimum—the method is designed to be highly structured, not confessional or storytelling.
- We do not give examples concerning anyone else in the group, whether they are in attendance or not.
- Whatever is said in this group, stays in this group and is not to be discussed outside.

Excuse, don't accuse others or yourself. – *Negative judgements hurt others and yourself.*

Meeting Etiquette

- We are group-minded and treat each other with respect.
- No "crosstalk" between attendees—focus on the example and the leader.
- If on a phone or online meeting, keep yourself muted until it's your turn to speak.
- Do not expand or add to an example—keep it brief, and do not elaborate on circumstances or personalities involved.
- Do not discuss sensitive subjects such as medication, sex, politics, religion or legal issues.
- No reading or sharing of materials from other programs or therapy texts.
- No religious materials, texts, or prayers during meetings—people from all denominations are welcome and included in RI meetings.
- We do not offer advice on medications, diagnoses or treatments or on how to handle a situation.
- No eating during a meeting—wait until after the meeting is over during the mutual aid/social time.
- Informal discussions and sharing of ideas and stories are encouraged during the mutual aid time, after the formal meeting is concluded.

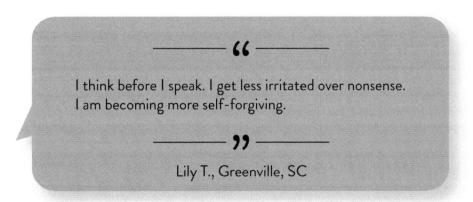

> I think before I speak. I get less irritated over nonsense. I am becoming more self-forgiving.
>
> Lily T., Greenville, SC

The Peer Leader Role

People in the group may be asked to take turns leading examples. Leading an example is not passive—when it's your turn, keep these things in mind:

During the **Example**, the leader:

- Reads or asks someone else to read each of the four parts of the example
- Listens to the example giver to hear when each part ends
- Makes sure each part of the example is covered
- Helps the example giver stay on the subject of each part
- Makes sure that the group does not talk during the example.

During the **Comment Period** the leader:

- Watches for and calls on group members' raised hands
- Relates each "tool" back to the example
- Makes sure the example giver does not talk during the comments
- Maintains order in the group: no cross-talking directly to the example giver or side conversations between participants.

If you are interested in Peer Leader training or in opening a new group, talk with your local Group or Area Leader or contact our main office through info@recoveryinternational.org

---

You have the power to choose what to believe or not believe. – *Once we know our fear and anger are just beliefs, we can replace them with realistic thoughts.*

Appendix A: Tool Lists

> It has made all the difference in my marriage and other relationships, enabled me to complete graduate work, hold a job and get along better with co-workers, as well as greatly improve my food-related behaviors.
>
> Ellie S., Aurora, IL

> It has undoubtedly saved our marriage, improved my social skills, caused me to be more tolerant and forgiving, and able to focus on the good rather than the negative of a situation.
>
> Eugene N., Reno, NV

Tool List

These tools are quoted or adapted from Dr. Low's books: *Mental Health Through Will Training*, *Selections from Dr. Low's Works*, and *Manage Your Fears, Manage Your Anger*. Many other tools can be found in these books, and the wording may vary slightly throughout his writings.

REINFORCE (Things to DO)

1. After the initial startle, then work yourself down.
2. Anticipate calmly.
3. Assert yourself without temper.
4. Bear discomfort and comfort will come.
5. Be group-minded not self-minded.
6. Be satisfied with small gains.
7. Be self-led, not symptom-led.
8. Calm begets calm, temper begets temper.
9. Carry the inner smile of self- approval.
10. Change your insecure thoughts to secure thoughts.
11. Choose peace over power.
12. Command your muscles to do what the brain fears to do.
13. Control your speech muscles.
14. Decide, plan and act.
15. Do the things you fear or hate to do.
16. Drop the judgement.
17. Drop your excessive sense of responsibility.
18. Endorse for each effort, not just the outcome.
19. Endorse rather than indict yourself and others.
20. Every act of self-control leads to a greater sense of self-respect.
21. Excuse, don't accuse others or yourself.
22. Face, tolerate and endure discomfort.
23. Feelings and sensations cannot be controlled, but thoughts and impulses can.
24. Feelings should be expressed and temper suppressed.
25. Have the courage to make mistakes in the trivialities of everyday life.
26. Have the will to effort, not the will to comfort.
27. Have the will to persevere.

28. If you can't decide, any decision will steady you.
29. If you lower your expectations, your performance will rise.
30. Impulses can be controlled.
31. It takes two to fight, one to lay down the sword.
32. Let go of wanting to please everybody.
33. Long-range goals call for patience and perseverance.
34. Objectivity can wipe out emotionalism.
35. Remove yourself from a tense and provoking situation.
36. Replace an insecure thought with a secure thought.
37. Self-endorsement creates a feeling of security.
38. Self-endorsement leads to self- respect.
39. Spot "imagination on fire."
40. Spot "racing thoughts."
41. Spot what is average.
42. Strive for peace, order and calm.
43. Symptoms can be patiently borne, bravely faced and humbly tolerated.
44. Take a total view rather than a partial view.
45. Take secure thoughts.
46. Thoughts and impulses alone are subject to control.
47. Thoughts can be suppressed, dropped or changed.
48. To stop an impulse, command your muscles not to act.
49. Treat mental health as a business, not as a game.
50. Try, fail, try, fail, try, succeed!
51. Until you regain control, "wear the mask."
52. Use motionless sitting.
53. We can break old habit patterns.
54. We can decide which thoughts to think.
55. We can decide which words to use.
56. We can only control our inner environment's reaction to outer environment.
57. We cannot endorse and indict ourselves at the same time.
58. We endorse even our smallest efforts.
59. When feeling overwhelmed, do things in "part acts."
60. You can't change a situation, but you can change your attitude towards it.

REFRAIN (Things to STOP Doing)

1. Anti-social responses must not be expressed.
2. A symbolic victory is a hollow victory.
3. Do not go for the "symbolic victory."
4. Don't expect to be comfortable in an uncomfortable situation.
5. Don't look regretfully into the past or fearfully into the future.
6. Don't take yourself too seriously.
7. Expectations can lead to disappointments.
8. Fearful anticipation is often worse than the realization
9. If you can't anticipate securely, then don't anticipate.
10. Self-appointed expectations can lead to self-induced frustrations.
11. Temper brings on tenseness.
12. Temper is blindness to the other side of the story.
13. Tempers are frequently uncontrolled, not uncontrollable.
14. Tenseness maintains and intensifies symptoms.
15. There are no uncontrollable impulses, only those you don't yet know how to control.
16. You can't bear someone else's discomfort.

REFLECT (Things to THINK About)

1. A sense of averageness brings balance.
2. Comfort is a want, not a need.
3. Feelings and sensations rise and fall.
4. Feelings are not facts, they can lie to us.
5. Fear is a belief, beliefs can be changed.
6. Frustrations are tolerable, average and not emergencies.
7. Helplessness is not hopelessness.
8. Humor is our best friend, temper is our worst enemy.
9. Hurt feelings are just beliefs not shared.
10. Initial feelings and sensations cannot be controlled, but can be managed.
11. It is average to feel uncomfortable in an uncomfortable situation.
12. It's not that we cannot, it's that we care not to bear the discomfort.
13. Life is full of frustrations.
14. Move our muscles, change our minds.

15. Nervous people don't like change.
16. Nervous symptoms are distressing, but not dangerous.
17. Nervous symptoms are just innocent sensations of a nervous imbalance.
18. Our supreme goal is our mental health.
19. Our supreme task is self-discipline.
20. Our supreme value is inner peace.
21. Outer environment gets to inner environment over the bridge of temper.
22. People do things that annoy us, not necessarily to annoy us.
23. People hope to be exceptional and fear they are nothing but average.
24. Perfection is an illusion.
25. Sensations are distressing but not dangerous.
26. Setbacks are unavoidable.
27. Symptoms are temporary not permanent.
28. The outer environment can be rude, crude, and indifferent.
29. There is no right or wrong in the trivialities of daily life.
30. To know is not to know.
31. We can't control the outer environment.

These tools, or "spots," are shorthand for broader concepts found in Recovery books. We encourage reading and studying these to understand the ideas in context. As you learn, read, practice and explore further, you will discover more tools and become better at using them.

> By becoming more realistic, more balanced and more mature about life and living, I have become a better mother, wife, and friend.
>
> Marilyn R., Billings, MT

Appendix B: Glossary of Terms

> "Even though I've never been diagnosed with a mental health issue, when my mom was suffering from severe dementia, I would get worked up during our conversations. I used the RI tools to better manage my relationship with her."
>
> Angela S., Oak Brook, IL

> "Recovery International has given me my life and it has given me a philosophy to help me cope with everyday living. Today I continue to attend RI meetings and even train new peer leaders!"
>
> Celinda J., Los Angeles, CA

Glossary of Terms

Averageness: Most of what we experience in daily life is average, not exceptional. It is helpful to set realistic goals, and not expect perfection.

Bad Habits: Destructive behaviors that we do habitually and carelessly (i.e. crying habit, complaining habit, gossiping habit, sarcasm habit).

Group-minded: Thinking about what is best for your group (family, classmates, friends, etc.).

Good Habits: Positive behaviors that we learn to do automatically such as endorsing ourselves, exchanging insecure thoughts with more secure thoughts, or doing what we know we should do in spite of our discomfort.

Inner Environment: everything *inside* oneself including feelings, sensations, thoughts, and impulses.

> <u>Feelings:</u> Emotions such as anger, impatience, hatred, fear, worry, embarrassment, shame, and many more. You cannot control your initial feelings, but by changing your thoughts and impulses, other feelings will follow.
>
> <u>Sensations:</u> Physical responses such as blushing, racing heartbeats, tense muscles, teary eyes, and many more. You cannot control these initial sensations, but by changing your thoughts and impulses, other sensations will follow.
>
> <u>Thoughts:</u> Ideas produced by thinking, such as, "This is fun," "I can do this," "He is annoying," and so on. You *can* learn to change your thoughts.
>
> <u>Impulses:</u> What you first want to do, such as to punch, to run, to hug, to laugh, to yell, and so on. You can learn to control your impulses.

Outer Environment: everything *outside* oneself, including people, the weather, traffic, events, and the past.

Sabotage: Anything done that interferes with the goal of managing anger and fear, such as using temperamental language, not using the tools, or rebelling. When we ignore or choose not to practice what we have learned. When we do not do what is best for our mental health.

Self-endorsement: A mental "pat on the back," self-praise for effort in practicing the method, using tools, and controlling thoughts and impulses; recognizing the value of every effort regardless of the result.

Self-minded: Asserting individual rights and domination over someone else or those around you.

Spotting: Identifying a disturbing feeling, sensation, thought or impulse; then applying the tools. Learning to recognize when you are worked up and taking a look at your tempers and symptoms, then applying RI tools to control impulses, drop judgment and move muscles.

Symptoms: Physical reactions to fearful or angry temper. (i.e. lethargy, agitation, increased heart rate) Negative thoughts such as "I never do anything right," "What will they think of me…."

Temper: The judgment of right and wrong in everyday events. *(Note: This does not apply to legal, moral, or ethical issues.)*

> Angry Temper: Negative judgments directed against another person or situation. (i.e. They are wrong.) This can take the form of resentment, impatience, indignation, annoyance, irritation, disgust, hatred or rebellion.
>
> Fearful Temper: Negative judgments directed against oneself (i.e. I am wrong.) This can take the form of discouragement, preoccupation, worry, embarrassment, hopelessness or despair.

Temperamental deadlock: Quarreling over who is right and who is wrong in everyday situations. It becomes an angry standoff.

Temperamental language: Exaggerated, negative, or insecure descriptions of experiences. Also, all language that is alarming and defeating.

Tools/Spots: Short sentences or phrases that are used as reminders of the techniques and concepts we are learning and practicing.

Trivialities: The routine events and irritations of daily life. Most events are trivial when compared to the importance of our health (mental, spiritual, emotional, physical).

Vicious Cycle: Temper and tenseness that increase the length and intensity of feelings and sensations.

Vitalizing Cycle: Anticipation or preoccupation with positive emotions and thoughts, leading to a greater sense of vitality, peace, security and confidence.

Will or Will-power: The power to choose how you are going to act and what you are going to think.

Working ourselves up: When we take negative or distressing thoughts and impulses and escalate them.

Appendix C: Worksheets

> "I tell anyone I talk to that this is a brilliant method for learning tools and applying them to manage mental health! One of my siblings in particular found it remarkably helpful in dealing with her PTSD issues and in learning to communicate in more secure and healthy ways. It changed our relationship from night to day!"
>
> Bobby B., Key West, FL

> "I don't know what I would do without this program. I had no tools to deal with my anxiety, and was barely functioning until I started learning the method."
>
> Louis C., Long Beach, CA

Example Worksheet

Practice constructing an example from your own experience. Think of a trivial situation where you experienced angry or fearful temper. Write out each step in the space below. Be brief and objective.

Step 1: Report a single situation or event that occurred - an everyday event when you began to work yourself up. Focus on a brief description of what happened: specifically, what triggered temper and symptoms? Indicate that you have finished this step by writing: "That's when I began to get worked up..."

_____

_____

_____

Step 2: Report the symptoms you experienced-both physical and mental. *(For instance, angry and fearful thoughts, confusion, palpitations, disturbing impulses, tightness in your chest, lowered feelings, sweaty palms, and so on.)*

_____

_____

_____

Step 3: Report your spotting of fearful and angry temper, the Recovery International tools you used to help yourself, and your self-endorsement for your effort.

_____

_____

_____

Step 4: Begin with "Before I had my Recovery training," and describe the temperamental reaction and symptoms you would have experienced in former days. What would have happened then versus what happened now?

_____

_____

_____

Endorse yourself for your effort or any improvement.

Example Worksheet

Practice constructing an example from your own experience. Think of a trivial situation where you experienced angry or fearful temper. Write out each step in the space below. Be brief and objective.

Step 1: Report a single situation or event that occurred - an everyday event when you began to work yourself up. Focus on a brief description of what happened: specifically, what triggered temper and symptoms? Indicate that you have finished this step by writing: "That's when I began to get worked up..."

_____

_____

_____

Step 2: Report the symptoms you experienced-both physical and mental. *(For instance, angry and fearful thoughts, confusion, palpitations, disturbing impulses, tightness in your chest, lowered feelings, sweaty palms, and so on.)*

_____

_____

_____

Step 3: Report your spotting of fearful and angry temper, the Recovery International tools you used to help yourself, and your self-endorsement for your effort.

_____

_____

_____

Step 4: Begin with "Before I had my Recovery training," and describe the temperamental reaction and symptoms you would have experienced in former days. What would have happened then versus what happened now?

_____

_____

_____

Endorse yourself for your effort or any improvement.

Example Worksheet

Practice constructing an example from your own experience. Think of a trivial situation where you experienced angry or fearful temper. Write out each step in the space below. Be brief and objective.

Step 1: Report a single situation or event that occurred - an everyday event when you began to work yourself up. Focus on a brief description of what happened: specifically, what triggered temper and symptoms? Indicate that you have finished this step by writing: "That's when I began to get worked up…"

_____

_____

_____

Step 2: Report the symptoms you experienced-both physical and mental. *(For instance, angry and fearful thoughts, confusion, palpitations, disturbing impulses, tightness in your chest, lowered feelings, sweaty palms, and so on.)*

_____

_____

_____

Step 3: Report your spotting of fearful and angry temper, the Recovery International tools you used to help yourself, and your self-endorsement for your effort.

_____

_____

_____

Step 4: Begin with "Before I had my Recovery training," and describe the temperamental reaction and symptoms you would have experienced in former days. What would have happened then versus what happened now?

_____

_____

_____

Endorse yourself for your effort or any improvement.

Example Worksheet

Practice constructing an example from your own experience. Think of a trivial situation where you experienced angry or fearful temper. Write out each step in the space below. Be brief and objective.

Step 1: Report a single situation or event that occurred - an everyday event when you began to work yourself up. Focus on a brief description of what happened: specifically, what triggered temper and symptoms? Indicate that you have finished this step by writing: "That's when I began to get worked up…"

_____

_____

_____

Step 2: Report the symptoms you experienced-both physical and mental. *(For instance, angry and fearful thoughts, confusion, palpitations, disturbing impulses, tightness in your chest, lowered feelings, sweaty palms, and so on.)*

_____

_____

_____

Step 3: Report your spotting of fearful and angry temper, the Recovery International tools you used to help yourself, and your self-endorsement for your effort.

_____

_____

_____

Step 4: Begin with "Before I had my Recovery training," and describe the temperamental reaction and symptoms you would have experienced in former days. What would have happened then versus what happened now?

_____

_____

_____

Endorse yourself for your effort or any improvement.

Appendix D:
The History of Recovery International

> "
> I was able to recover from my initial illness, get married and have children. I have had two setbacks since being in Recovery and thanks to the method, I worked through them. Through the use of spotting and tools I have improved in social situations.
> "
>
> Jesus P., Miami, FL

> "
> RI has been extremely helpful. It has completely changed my life for the better. It has helped me to control panic attacks, compulsive overeating, and numerous other problems that affected my mental health.
> "
>
> Sonny G., Seattle, WA

Dr. Abraham Low

Born in Poland, Abraham Low graduated from the University of Strasbourg in 1913 and completed medical school at the University of Vienna in 1919. He obtained his license to practice psychoanalysis in 1922 in New York, and in 1925 joined the staff at the University of Illinois Medical School. He later became head of staff and then acting director of the University's Psychiatric Institute, and supervised the Illinois State Psychiatric Hospitals for more than a decade.

In 1937, Dr. Low and a group of patients formed an organization to help people leaving hospitalization re-enter society and eliminate the stigma of mental illness. He saw the need to develop a consistent, supportive treatment approach that could be replicated by non-professionals, which led to 25 years of cognitive behavioral work and peer leader training. This, along with numerous books and lectures evolved into the Recovery Method.

When Dr. Low died in 1954, his wife, daughters, and hundreds of dedicated patients and volunteers carried on his work. More than one million people have been helped to lead more peaceful and productive lives using these techniques.

The efficacy of the method has been studied many times over the years and, in 2000, the American Psychiatric Association recognized Recovery's contribution to the field with the Arnold L. Van Amerigen Award in Psychiatric Rehabilitation.*

Dr. Low's personal letters and manuscripts, along with early Recovery publications, are housed at the University of Illinois in the Special Collections and University Archives Reading Room at the Library of the Health Sciences–Chicago. Please contact lib-spec@uic.libanswers.com or call 312-996-8977.

*For professional articles and studies, visit recoveryinternational.org and select the Professionals page.

Recovery International

In the 1930's, the state-of-the-art treatment for mental illness was electric shock treatment. Cold water immersion, insulin shock and lobotomies were other remedies for those with recurrent "nervous" disorders. The stigma of mental illness was compounded in states like Illinois, where one received a court record when released from a state hospital.

Recovery was founded in 1937 by Dr. Abraham Low and his patients—people who knew that mental illness was not a permanent sentence to the sidelines of life. They fought for the ability to talk openly about their conditions, to talk about recovery, to talk about eliminating the stigma of a mental illness diagnosis.

They faced this stigma very early on, as the group was originally called *"The Association of Nervous and Former Mental Patients."* After one of their members was evicted from his rooming house because he received a letter with the Association's return address, they changed the name to Recovery, Inc. As meetings expanded across the country and then abroad, the name was changed to Recovery International. Recovery International currently operates hundreds of meetings per week in communities, online and through telephone conference calls.

Now, there are thousands of organizations dedicated to promoting mental health all over the world. Peer leaders are now recognized as helpful aides to professional treatment. We are proud to be the "granddaddy" of this movement, and proud to still be here more than 80 years later—helping people with depression, anxiety, and other conditions live better lives using Dr. Low's method.

One thing we have learned is that mental health is for *everybody*. According to Mental Health America, one in five people will experience a mental health condition sometime during their life, and a high percentage of those will experience chronic, ongoing issues. Recovery support meetings have helped more than a million people manage their symptoms, and there are lessons to be learned in the Recovery Method that can help *anyone* deal better with the ups and downs of daily living.

> **Drop your excessive sense of responsibility.** – *You are not responsible for others, and you can't do everything perfectly.*

Recovery's Self-Help Method

The Better. Mental. Health. *for Everyone* workbook is designed to introduce the basic concepts of the Recovery Method in a simple and engaging way. These can help anyone manage stress and anger more effectively. For many people suffering from chronic mental health issues, the Recovery Method provides evidence-based, self-help techniques that can relieve symptoms and help them lead more peaceful and productive lives.

The Recovery Method was developed by Dr. Abraham Low over the course of many years working with patients hospitalized for mental health treatments, outpatients, and private practice patients. Key elements of the method as defined by Dr. Low include:[1]

1. <u>Residual Symptoms & Vicious Cycle</u> – After leaving hospitalization, nervous patients can still experience vicious cycles of symptoms (fatigue, sleeplessness, headaches, etc.) increasing fear and these fears perpetuating the symptoms. This cycle can be broken by addressing the symptoms using Recovery tools.

2. <u>Chronic Neuroses & Defeatism</u> – Even long-term suffering can be relieved by enduring initial sensations and controlling impulses. Peer leaders demonstrate that chronic conditions are not hopeless.

3. <u>Setbacks</u> – Participants should plan to attend Recovery meetings or use the method on their own for at least six months. It takes time and practice to learn how to internalize and apply the tools. Setbacks are to be expected.

4. <u>Symptomatic Idiom</u> –Symptoms aim to convey a sense of danger, and to suggest the worst-case scenario of physical or mental collapse leading to permanent handicap. Learn to avoid alarmist, incendiary and defeatist language by using Recovery language and tools.

5. <u>Temper and Temperamental Lingo</u> – Angry or aggressive temper happens when you feel someone else has done you wrong. This leads to resentment, impatience, indignation, disgust, hatred, and even violence. Fearful temper arises when you feel you are wrong or you think someone else is judging you as being wrong. This causes you to retreat and feel discouraged, embarrassed, shamed, inadequate, hopeless, despair, etc. Both these types of tempers reinforce and intensify symptoms, which increases the reaction, leading to a vicious cycle. Additionally, certain terms incite a temperamental response, so one must learn to avoid certain words and replace them with more neutral and positive ones.

[1] Note: The original Concise Outline of Recovery's Self-Help Techniques, was written by Dr. Abraham Low for the second edition of *Mental Health Through Will Training* in 1952.

6. <u>Recovery Language</u> – Recovery Language is designed to counteract symptomatic idiom and temperamental lingo. Key points include "sabotage" and "authority." In short, patients often sabotage the authority of the physician and must practice to overcome this habit.

7. <u>Spotting Technique</u> – Participants must constantly and consistently practice "Spotting" in order to reject the symptomatic idiom and temperamental lingo and curtail the symptom or reaction.

For those who wish to delve deeper into the Recovery program, case studies and examples illustrating these and other key concepts appear in Dr. Low's books, articles, and lectures. We suggest attendance at Recovery Meetings to learn the Method, and encourage further reading to understand the concepts and "spots" in context.

Appendix E:
Books by and about Dr. Abraham Low and Recovery International

Books by and about Dr. Abraham Low and Recovery International

The origins and ideas behind the tools and this method can be found in the following books:

Manage Your Fears, Manage Your Anger by Abraham A. Low, M.D.– Transcriptions of Low's 70 taped lectures from 1953 and 1954. (First published 1995; Third Edition, 2019.)

Mental Health Through Will Training by Abraham A. Low, M.D.– primary text of Low's work used at Recovery International meetings. (First published 1950; Fourth Edition, 2019.)

Mental Illness, Stigma and Self-Help, The Founding of Recovery, Inc. – This book describes the early development of Recovery International. (First published as *The Historical Development of Recovery's Self-Help Project*, 1943; Second Edition, 1991)

My Dear Ones, Neil and Margaret Rau – Biography of Dr. Abraham Low and Recovery International. (First published 1971; Reprinted 1990)

Peace vs. Power In The Family: Domestic Discord and Emotional Distress by Abraham A. Low, M.D.– Writings focused on family dynamics. (First published as *Lectures to Relatives of Former Patients*, 1943; Third Edition, 2014.)

Selections from Dr. Low's Work by Abraham A. Low, M.D. – Writings from 1950 to 1953 that include additional insights for practicing the Recovery International Method. (Published in full,1953; Third Edition, 2019.)

The Wisdom of Dr. Low – Compilation of Low's inspiring words in an easy reference format to help with a current problem or for daily affirmations. (First Published 2009; Second Edition 2019.)

To purchase books or to become a member of Recovery International visit recoveryinternational.org.

Made in the USA
Coppell, TX
10 July 2022

79783300R00061